D1554497

SHREE SHIRDI SAI BABA
OF
SOUTH SAN FRANCISCO

DIVINE TOUCH

OTHER TITLES BY BEYOND MAYA PRESS

BHAROSHA MA: 22 WEEKS WITH DIVINITY (2009)

All of these titles are available at **gwynmcgee.com**

SHREE SHIRDI SAI BABA
OF
SOUTH SAN FRANCISCO

DIVINE TOUCH

Anita Bawa & Gwyn McGee

Beyond Maya Press

BEYOND MAYA PRESS   Beyond Maya Press

SHREE SHIRDI SAI BABA of South San Francisco: DIVINE TOUCH

Cover Design: Steve L. Patterson

Interior photos/images: Steve L. Patterson, Naveen Goswami, Maria Crane, Melisha Ram, Larry McGee, and author, Gwyn McGee

ISBN: 978-0-9834270-0-1

DEDICATION
Anita Bawa and Gwyn McGee

This book is dedicated to Shree Shirdi Sai Baba for being the greatest Guru and Fakir.

ACKNOWLEDGEMENTS
by Anita Bawa

First... foremost, I'd like to bow to Shree Shirdi Sai Baba's feet for fulfilling the goal of writing this book and allowing me to share my experiences and dreams with others. Thanks BABA for sending a wonderful writer, editor, and publisher-Gwyn McGee.

I'd like to thank my parents, Mohinder Pal Bawa and Simla Bawa, who believed in me and allowed me to experience different religions and always supported me and reminded me that GOD is one although we may call Him/Her by different names.

I would like to thank my husband, Naveen Goswami, who encouraged and supported me in writing this book.

I also want to thank my son Aaron Goswami, and my daughter Sarah Goswami, for listening to my stories and dreams.

I want to thank Maria Crane for her special guidance on spirituality and sharing her books on BABA.

Lastly, for all the family members and friends who provided their stories to share in this book, a great thanks goes out to you.

GYARAH VACHAN
The Eleven Sayings of Shirdi Sai Baba

~ Whoever puts his feet on Shirdi soil, his sufferings would come to an end.

~ The wretched and miserable would rise into plenty of joy and happiness as soon as they climb the steps of my Samadhi.

~ I shall be ever active and vigorous even after leaving this earthly body.

~ My tomb shall bless and speak to the needs of my devotees.

~ I shall be active and vigorous even from the tomb.

~ My mortal remains would speak from the tomb.

~ I am ever living to help and guide all who come to me, who surrender to me, and who seek refuge in me.

~ If you look to me, I look to you.

~ If you cast your burden on me, I shall surely bear it.

~ If you seek my advice and help, it shall be given to you at once.

~ There shall be no want in the house of my devotees.

INTRODUCTION

On October 2nd, 2010 the stretch of Highway 1 between Santa Cruz, California and South San Francisco felt longer than it had ever been. I was in a hurry, and all I could see was an endless stream of car lights. Obviously I was aware of the drive but one thought truly consumed me: Shirdi Sai Baba was waiting for me in South San Francisco. In my heart there was no doubt about that. I could feel it. My mind on the other hand was not as easily convinced. Inside my mind I kept repeating, 'Baba, ple-ease wait for me. Please Baba, wait.'

Now… you're probably asking how I can say Shirdi Sai Baba was waiting for me, Anita Bawa, in the year 2010, when he took his Samadhi…that is…made his transition on October 15, 1918? How could I ask him to wait? And of all the places in the world South San Francisco, California in the United States. Not Shirdi or Puttaparthi in India.

I can say this because Sai Baba comes to South San Francisco. He does. Baba gives darshan in South San Francisco in a very special way, through a very special person. His divine touch comes upon her. I am saying Shirdi Sai Baba incorporates into this unique being. She becomes Shirdi Sai Baba.

Now for those of you who are not open to the possibility of Sai Baba coming through another human body in this manner I respect your position, but it does not alter the reality of what is occurring in South San Francisco.

Once J. Jagadeesan, author of the Sai Baba: Journey To God Series, asked Sathya Sai Baba to bless a book in the collection entitled The Fourth Dimension. In Baba's presence Jagadeesan pleaded, after he experienced two particularly powerful trance mediums, for Baba to tell him if this kind of phenomenon was real. Jagadeesan wrote about his conversation with Sathya Sai Baba in the book The Fourth Dimension.

Jaga: Bhagavan, I know you have talked against this whole phenomenon of trance. (Jagadeesan speaks of a particular case before he spoke of)…a girl who at that time was manifesting an incredibly powerful trance phenomenon of Shakti, "Divine Mother"… I cannot believe these are false! Please Bhagavan (I pleaded) tell me what is true!

Baba: (smiling gently and sensing the earnestness of my query replied) "Yes! This is true! But do you know why Swami discourages? Because for every truth there are a hundred false."

Sathya Sai Baba confirmed there are some people who have this unique ability, and there are more who claim to have it but do not.

What is occurring in South San Francisco is real. Through my experiences I have also come to accept and have been humbled by the sheer complexity of Sai Baba. He can not be understood by the human mind alone. To embrace Sai Baba the heart is key. This book is an account of a portion of my heartfelt journey with Baba.

It was made known to me in December, 2004 that I would write a book about Baba's experiences in South San Francisco. I say 'made known to me' because… let me be very clear; I am not a writer. The thought of writing a book made me very nervous. Through the years I had witnessed Baba's words always came true, so Baba's declaration that I would write a book left me scared and wondering how this would be possible. But in spite of my fear and hesitation I began to take notes about various Baba experiences in South San Francisco. For 10 years, I wrote notes and included some of my dreams in the notebooks as I waited for the right moment; the time when my collection would be made into a book.

There is a quote from Shirdi Sai Baba in the book, **SHRI SAI SATCHARITA,** *The Wonderful Life And Teachings Of Shri Sai Baba* that referred to the author, 'Hemadpant'; a quote that I now fully understand: "Let him make a collection of stories and experiences, keep notes and memos, I will help him. **He is only an outward instrument. I should write My autobiography Myself and satisfy the wishes of My devotees.**"

It was not until I read *Bharosha Ma: 22 Weeks With Divinity* written by Gwyn McGee, a veteran author of nineteen years, that an interesting chain of events took place.

First, I met Gwyn in February of 2010. Where did I meet her? In South San Francisco; in the mandir where Sai Baba gives darshan. From the beginning there was a definite chemistry between us and soon we began to feel that she might play a key role in the book that I was asked to write six years earlier. Because of the synchronicities Gwyn and I entertained the thought that we may have been given a particular role in one of Baba's countless *lilas*…His divine plays. This lila: the creation of this book, Shree Shirdi Sai Baba of South San Francisco: Divine Touch.

CHAPTER ONE

Jagpal Gosain, my cousin, introduced me to Sai Baba but it was my husband, Naveen, who opened our lives to the world of Sai Baba. Naveen was the engine behind our spiritual enthusiasm. I have never seen myself as a *puja* person; a person who is deep into spiritual ceremonies or prayers. In some ways I still don't. I am a researcher by profession, a manager for a highly respected biotechnology company, and spirituality was simply not on my radar.

Naveen was different. It was Naveen who brought the first photograph of Sai Baba into our home; a photo of Sathya Sai Baba. I find it rather interesting how Baba determined it would be experiences with Him as Shirdi Sai Baba that actually changed our lives.

On May 25, 2000, Naveen and I found ourselves looking for the street where Jagpal informed us Sai *bhajans* were being held every Thursday. We lived in Daly City and the bhajans took place in South San Francisco; a city with which we were not familiar. We drove from street to street, that evening, before we finally found our destination. We knew it was the right house because we could hear singing inside.

After Naveen and I walked up to the door we knocked, but there was no answer. Not knowing what else to do we turned the knob and the door opened. Immediately, we knew the devotional singing was coming from upstairs so we mounted the stairs, quietly, and followed the sound. When we arrived in the room at the top, Naveen joined the men who sat in front of an altar on one side, and I sat down on the other side with the women.

There were approximately fifteen people in the small, narrow space. They all focused on a modest altar located in front of us in the middle of the room. Many Hindu deities were displayed on the wooden structure, and my curiosity was piqued by the presence of *vibhuti*, a kind of ash, in a variety of colors. There was also *ghee* and a syrupy liquid which I later found out was *amrit*. These substances were on some of the photographs, pictures, and statues. A pleasant surprise was an abundance of *misri*, rock candy, on a statue of Ganesh. After I perused the altar I continued to study the room. To my left was a sink, and I got the feeling when bhajans were not being held the room performed double duty as a kitchen.

As I mentioned before, I am probably not your typical puja person, but I must say my heart was touched by the young couple who seemed to lead the bhajans. Initially, I sat in silence and observed what was going on. In my life I have heard devotional Hindu songs before. Being a native of India, although I left and came to the United States when I was fourteen years old, how could I not? So it didn't take long before I concluded I was among people whose ancestors were from the Fiji Island. It was the way the songs were delivered.

I enjoyed the singing, but the truth to be told Naveen was more interested in bhajans and Baba than I was at that time. We stayed until the end, but we left without saying a word to anyone.

After two weeks we returned and again I quietly participated. But this time before we could make a silent escape the female of the couple, who appeared to be in charge, stopped us.

She was very beautiful and wore an exquisite sari with bangles and earrings that perfectly matched. Her skin was a flawless, lovely shade of light brown that contrasted becomingly against her black hair which hung just below her shoulders. But it was the woman's eyes that stood out. Her eyes were very dark and captivating. I am 5'3", and I had to look up slightly into those eyes when she spoke, so I guessed she was perhaps 5'7" tall.

"Why didn't you stay for dinner the last time?" she asked.

"We didn't know there was dinner," Naveen replied.

"We had no idea," I chimed in.

Immediately she said, "Come with me," and she led us to a kitchen downstairs. "My name is Shree Lal, but you can call me Malthi."

"I'm Naveen Goswami, and this is my wife, Anita," Naveen made the introductions.

From there, with Malthi and the other attendees, we shared a meal of rice, vegetables, and roti. Although it was my first time joining them in such a fashion; I distinctly felt as if I had known them before. We chatted for a short while and names were shared, but I didn't recall most of them after we left and returned home to Daly City.

All in all it was a very pleasant experience, and we began to attend bhajans on a regular basis. I found I was glad for the upliftment I felt I received. You see, it was a trying time for Naveen and me as a couple, because of business problems. I believe we both found comfort there. Eventually, a woman named Sarita Dayal, who was quite friendly, reached out to me.

"How long have you known the Lal family?" I asked one night as we ate the dinner the Lal's consistently provided after bhajans.

"I met them in 1984. Malthi was fifteen years old at the time. You know," Sarita, who was quite pretty, gazed off into the distance for a moment, "since I have known her Auntie has always been very religious."

I realized Sarita referred to Malthi's mother, Parvati, as Auntie.

"Parvati Auntie has been a devotee of Sai Baba since you have known her?" I asked, wanting to know more.

"Yes. I recall some years ago she went home to Fiji. When she returned she brought back three t-shirts with Sathya Sai Baba on them. Auntie said He was God."

Baba is God? I thought. *Is that what they think?* I held that thought in my mind as I continued to listen to what Sarita had to say.

"They have been holding Sai bhajans on and off in their home since 1988."

I was somewhat surprised to discover the Lal family had been holding bhajans for twelve years before we met them. Why? The bhajans felt very intimate. It didn't feel like an event that had been going on for that long. There was a sense of family among the small group that attended bhajans religiously, and Naveen and I began to feel we belonged.

The more we came, and the more we lingered and chatted after bhajans, the more we learned about the Lal family. There was Parvati Auntie, Malthi's mother, Ram Lal Uncle, her father, and Dhiren, her husband. There was also Roshini, her sister, and Malthis' two children Justin, who was nine, and Kushbu who was about three years old. There were several others who seemed to be very close to the Lal family including a young man named Asish Chandra, who appeared to be a teenager. He was not the only youth who attended the bhajans faithfully, and it was wonderful to see such young people willingly involved in puja.

Shree 'Malthi' Lal

CHAPTER TWO

At some point I began to notice something unusual was happening in the midst of bhajans, and it centered on Malthi. Week after week I had a clear view of her profile as I sat propped against the wall perhaps five feet away. Over time I couldn't help but notice about forty minutes after the Sai bhajans began subtle changes occurred in Malthi's facial expression. Malthi looked different. I don't know how to explain it, but there was a definite change in her and I knew something was happening. Once the changes began I also noticed Malthi stopped singing. Now it may seem like a leap to you, the reader, but based on my observation of her movements and the changes in her face I began to think, *this is not Malthi*. No one had ever said that to me, but I came to that conclusion. Perhaps it is something you have to see to truly understand.

Once again I need to be clear…I have never considered that this kind of thing could take place. I had not considered it because I had no interest in the subject of trance mediumship. My background is; I am a researcher/scientist. My world is about physical facts and evidence. It was the changes in Malthi that I witnessed, call it evidence if you will, that caused me to entertain the thought that Malthi was no longer Malthi...that sometimes during bhajans she became someone or something else. If I hadn't been sitting so close week after week the thought probably would not have occurred to me. But I sat very close to her and I had never seen that kind of transformation in another human being. The changes I saw in Malthi created a battle in my mind as to how this kind of thing might happen. Could it actually happen?

One night after bhajans I was determined to find out what was going on. I approached Asish, who we all call Ashu, with the subject. Naveen was with me.

"Ashu, I want to ask you something," I began.

His smooth brow creased a bit. "Okay."

"What was happening when Matlhi stop singing in the middle of that bhajan?"

Ashu's bright eyes beamed a calm sincerity. "Bhaini is very close to Shirdi Sai Baba and He comes," he replied without hesitation. "He takes over her body."

"What???" I looked at Naveen. Then I looked back at Ashu. Although I thought something like that was going on I was still surprised to hear Ashu say it.

"Yes. She is a very special person," Ashu continued. "I have known her for twelve years and I know that Baba comes."

I stared at this young man who had validated my suspicions. The truth is I still wondered if it was true. But then I thought, *if it isn't true, why would they pretend such a thing?* Naveen and I had attended bhajans for months and no one had mentioned this phenomenon was occurring, so I knew they weren't benefiting from what would have been a silent hoax.

Finally I replied rather lamely, "Malthi has a very interesting life."

"Her life is interesting," Ashu said, "and it has been very challenging."

"In what way?" I asked.

"In many ways," he replied, "but especially when it comes to sickness. My sister has suffered all kinds of sicknesses since she was nine years old. Baba said He has been physically with Bhayani since that time." Ashu was quiet for a moment before he continued. "I'm not sure if all of the sickness that has been a part of her life is her sickness or if she is taking on the illnesses of others to help them."

~ "I have to suffer for My devotees, their difficulties are Mine" ~ Shri Sai Satcharita - pg. 44

What a strange thing to say, I thought. "How does Baba speak to Malthi?"

"From what I understand He is in constant communication with her. She can hear Him within her mind."

Well…. I heard what Ashu said; I saw what I saw; but finally my mind could not accept that Shirdi Sai Baba was coming into Malthi and she was no longer Malthi but actually Shirdi Sai Baba. That was too long of a stretch for me.

That night as we drove home after bhajans, Naveen and I had quite a conversation.

"Do you really think Baba comes in another human being?" I asked Naveen.

At the time I was unfamiliar with the quote from Shirdi Sai Baba in the Shri Sai Satcharita, **"Believe Me, though I pass away, My bones in My tomb would be speaking, moving and communicating with those, who would surrender themselves whole-heartedly to Me."**

"Ye-es," was Naveen's solid reply.

I could tell from my husband's face he believed this was possible, and he believed it was happening in front of his eyes in South San Francisco.

"Re-ally?" I struggled with the whole trance medium concept and process. I needed facts and data and I didn't have enough of it regardless of the changes I witnessed in Malthi. I guess what I am attempting to convey is, I believed in God but not in trance mediumship. You might think because we had been going to bhajans for months and I had been witnessing those changes in Malthi that Naveen and I would have talked about this subject before I approached Ashu. But at the time bhajans was a one day a week moment, and we were dealing with what felt like larger life issues. That is simply the way it was.

"I have seen vibhuti appearing on pictures and statues before," Naveen proclaimed as we rode in the car.

"You have?" I was really surprised.

"Yes, in Punjab, India. In Patalia, when I was little growing up there. So I recognize what is going on in their home."

What could I say? I had no experience with this kind of thing. Perhaps Naveen had not said anything before because he knew I viewed life through a "scientific" lens. Maybe he felt I had no desire to know such things as manifested vibhuti existed, and that I might not accept it had he told me. Naveen was probably right. So, in light of these things I kept my doubts to myself.

Baba's robe and sandals materializing
vibhuti: 2002

CHAPTER THREE

We continued to go to bhajans and my uncertainty about Malthi continued as well. One day when I got the chance I asked Sarita what she knew.

"There is a deep history in this family with Baba on both Malthi's mother and father's side," Sarita calmly began. "When Malthi was young her father's sister, who was very close to Baba, gave Malthi a Durga."

"Ashu told me Baba said He has been with her since she was nine years old."

"I think I've heard that before. So there has been something special about Malthi since she was a child," Sarita replied. "And Auntie has always been full of faith. She started bhajans in 1988 in the house they lived in when I met them. Bhajans were held on and off back then.

"Parvati Auntie started the bhajans?"

"Yes. This is who Auntie is. She is always busy preparing the mandir and the food for bhajans, taking care of Roshini and the family. She is an amazing woman," Sarita proclaimed then continued. "And when Malthi got sick with the brain tumor in 1991 they started holding bhajans all the time. Auntie went everywhere trying to help Malthi. It was very difficult for all of them." She sighed. "But I remember a man named Mr. Dayal gave Auntie a statue of Sathya Sai Baba around that time. The statue had a significant crack in it. Eventually that statue repaired itself."

There was so much in Sarita's few words that I grabbed on to the one thing that stood out for me. "The statue repaired itself?" I looked deep into Sarita's eyes and sought the truth.

"It did," she stated emphatically.

I was stunned. "When did Baba start coming, Sarita?"

"I believe Baba started coming in 1998," she replied.

"So Baba has been coming like this for two years?" Again I was surprised because it had only been three weeks since I had begun to pay specific attention to the changes in Malthi during bhajans.

"Yes it has been that long."

Sarita, who always wore a beautiful sari, adjusted the top of the garment, and for a moment I was aware of the western clothes I preferred the majority of the time.

"How did you know Baba was coming into Malthi?" I asked.

"One day Malthi was sitting in the front as she does now and she was singing a bhajan. Then all of a sudden she stopped singing in the middle of it. The next thing I knew Auntie picked up the bhajan."

"She started to sing where Malthi stopped," I said.

Sarita nodded. "Yes. Later when I spoke to Auntie about it she told me Baba was on her."

Was on her….I had never heard the expression. "You are saying Parvati Auntie knew what was happening to Malthi from the very beginning?"

"Yes," she nodded. "In Fiji we are familiar with this kind of thing."

~I shall be active and vigorous even from the tomb.~
Gyarah Vachan

Ashu, who had joined us a minute or so before said, "The first time Baba came I didn't know what was happening. All I knew was her facial expression changed. It changed a lot and I felt something was different. But at the time Bhayani had a brain tumor and I didn't know if what was happening to her face was a result of her being sick. What convinced me that Baba was coming was this." His vibrant eyes bore into me. "When I am at home praying, I always hold three flowers in my hands during the prayer. So one day I was standing behind Bhayani after bhajans, and suddenly she threw some flowers over her head and I was showered by the blossoms. Later she told me Baba told her 'Your brother always holds three flowers when he prays'." His face lit up. "That's when I knew Baba was coming into Bhayani. And I don't know if you've received any messages this way, Anita, but this is how Baba communicates with us because He doesn't speak when He's here," Ashu continued to explain. "He comes into my sister and when she comes back into her own consciousness she relays Baba's messages. Once my sister came back and told me Baba said when He was alive in Shirdi, I was Tatya."

I listened intently and I knew Naveen, Sarita and Ashu were convinced that Baba came into Malthi, but I must confess I still had my doubts.

Malthi, Kushbu and Anita in the mandir in 2001

THOSE WHO THINK THAT BABA
IS ONLY IN SHIRDI HAVE TOTALLY
FAILED TO KNOW ME.

Shirdi Sai Baba

CHAPTER FOUR

It was no more than one month later when the data I needed to convince me Shirdi Sai Baba actually came through Malthi was provided. I attended bhajans and sat in my usual spot to enjoy the devotional singing. Then once again it happened; from all indications Shirdi Sai Baba was there. This time to my utter surprise He motioned with His hand for me to come to Him.

Oh my God, why is he calling **me?** I thought. But I got up and kneeled in front of Him as He requested. Once I was there Baba picked up a white carnation and began to rub it between his fingers using a rapid, unusual motion. I watched the small blossom as He worked it that way, and right before my eyes a Lord Shiva locket appeared. It came from the middle of the delicate blossom.

I must tell you this. My parents and ancestors believe in Lord Shiva. Shiva is the only God that I grew up with. His, Lord Shiva, was the only picture of God that I had in my home during that time, and the Lord Shiva image that Shirdi Baba materialized was a small replica of that exact image.

I was totally shocked. Immediately the question came into

my mind, *How did He know that this deity was the only one my family prayed to?* I did not understand how Shirdi Baba knew. But for me the locket I held in my hand was proof that He knew. How many Gods do they say India has? Millions? No one knows for sure. But out of the possible millions of diety images, Shirdi Sai Baba materialized the exact and only image of God that hung on the walls of my house for many years. None of the Sai family members had been to our home so this was not publicly known. This event provided the data I needed. From that moment on I was certain it was Shirdi Sai Baba who sat in front of me. It was not Malthi.

Bhajans ended, and my Shiva locket was the talk of the night. Every time I looked at the locket I said, "I cannot believe it". But I had to believe it because I saw it materialize.

That night I had a very memorable conversation with Malthi. I approached her with the locket and said, "Look at what I got from Baba!" I held out my hand for her to see the locket, and I could tell from the look on Malthi's face she was as surprised as I was.

"Wo-oww! You got your favorite God. Are you going to wear this locket?"

I noticed Malthi knew Lord Shiva was my ancestral deity although I had never told her. "No, I won't", I replied, "Baba did not give me a locket that could be hung on a chain."

"If you like you could have a hook made," she suggested. "But knowing you, you will not, because you don't wear jewelry."

Malthi was absolutely right. I am not into wearing jewelry.

This was a turning point for me toward Shirdi Baba and the miracles He was unfolding in that house. It also opened my heart to the family. I began to feel I was truly a part of them.

The days and nights that followed were an energetic high.

For two nights I could not sleep. I'd lie awake wondering how this kind of thing could happen. How could physical objects simply materialize? I no longer doubted it occurred, but now I wondered about the higher power behind the miracle. Where did it exist? Was this magic? I knew the locket appeared, and I wondered if it would disappear since it was able to appear. For days I kept looking at my locket to ensure it was real. To this day I still have it with me.

During that time I had so much in my mind and in my heart. I wanted to know more. I needed to know, so I spoke to Sarita again after bhajans the following Thursday.

"Did you know Baba materialized a locket for me during bhajans last week? He gave me Shiva."

Sarita smiled. "That's really good. This is an amazing place," she said. "So much goes on here. For awhile now Auntie has been sharing things with me that happen in their home on Thursdays even before the bhajans." Sarita spoke with enthusiasm. "Miracles happen all the time, Anita, and for me one of the most interesting ones is the smell that comes from Malthi's feet."

"What did you say?" I thought I heard her correctly but I had to be sure.

Sarita smiled a full, yet gentle smile. "An absolutely beautiful scent comes from Malthi's feet on Thursdays."

I had no idea what kind of miracle Sarita was going to share but this…. "I've never heard of such a thing".

"It's true. Her feet have this wonderful scent of jasmine and more. I don't know what those scents are but they make this absolutely amazing smell." She continued to smile.

"I guess anything is possible," I replied because of my experience with the locket. "And there are so many manifestations on their altar. More things have come since

Naveen and I have been coming. There is more ghee on Krishna and definitely more misri on Ganesh. I have to say they are definitely blessed with Baba's grace," I found myself saying.

The locket Baba manifested for Anita and
the only image of Shiva in her home

CHAPTER FIVE

My amazement that Baba, with His divine touch on Malthi, had actually materialized a locket was only the beginning of this kind of phenomenon in our lives. To believe that Baba was present in Malthi at bhajans because of physical changes in her was one thing; for Baba to materialize objects while he was present in Malthi elevated the phenomenon to another level. It made me believe anything was possible; that there was a reality existing beyond the physical laws of science. Naveen and I were able to experience that reality because of Malthi. We had truly become fond of her, and fond of the Lal family.

One day we decided to invite her to our house. I knew Malthi and some of her family had visited the homes of other Sai family members, and Naveen and I wanted to share the prayer room we had created with her. We called Malthi and to our delight she accepted the invitation. When the day arrived I was surprised to see Malthi standing outside our door, alone. It would be the first time we spent one-on-one time with her.

"Sai Ram, Malthi. Welcome to our home," Naveen said. "Please come in."

I welcomed her too before Naveen led the way to our prayer room.

Malthi entered the small room we had dedicated to Baba. "Your prayer room is beautiful," she said.

I looked at the life size picture of Sathya Sai Baba in the center of the cocktail table, the large decorative Shiva image mounted on the main wall in front of the room, and several small statues of Hindu Gods and Goddesses that we had meticulously brought together. But my gaze returned to one of my favorites displayed in a chair; a beautiful painting of Shirdi Sai Baba giving the blessing sign as he stood beside a stream. Flowers were at his feet, and brahmin cows were in the distance along with a gold temple and a flowering tree.

I watched Malthi kneel before she began to pray. I looked at Naveen and through eye communication we silently agreed to follow her lead, and before I knew it our little daughter, Sarah, had joined us. We probably prayed less than five minutes before we mimicked Malthi as she rose to her feet. But Malthi did not turn and address us, with a concentrated look she focused on Shirdi Sai Baba's image on the chair.

"Baba is here," Malthi said softly. "He is sitting on the chair."

I looked at the chair, but I couldn't see anything except the painting, and when I glanced at Naveen he didn't seem to see anything either.

"Sarah, can you see Baba sitting on the chair?" Malthi asked my six year old daughter.

Without hesitation Sarah replied, "Yes, I can see Baba. Baba is old and wearing old clothes."

I looked at my daughter and I thought *how lucky she is to have eyes that can see Baba*, and at that moment although I could not see Him, I could feel Baba's presence and His grace. I was also grateful to Malthi for making it happen.

"Malthi, would you like some tea or soft drink?" I offered as we left the room.

"Yes. I'll have a cup of tea," she replied.

We walked to the kitchen and I prepared the drink. When it was ready Malthi and Naveen drank tea and the three of us talked about Baba. Baba as a subject was still so new to Naveen and I that we could never talk about Him enough; and neither one of us wanted Malthi's visit to end.

"More tea, Malthi?" I offered.

"No thank you," she replied then motioned toward our prayer room. "Baba has blessed your house," Malthi announced.

I didn't know what her words meant but I knew something had occurred. Excited, I left the kitchen quickly and returned to the prayer room. I cannot explain my shock when I saw a large OM symbol made of vibhuti in the middle of Shirdi Sai Baba's heart ... the Shirdi Sai Baba image resting on the chair.

"Naveen! Malthi! Please come! You've got to see Baba's miracle!"

I didn't have to call out for long because they were close on my heels. With joy, I watched Naveen's face as he stared at the painting. Literally his jaw dropped and his mouth opened with surprise.

The gratitude I felt because Baba had blessed our home in such a way was extremely deep. I guess Naveen felt the same because in unison, without saying a word, we bowed in front of the chair that held His image.

Not long after the miracle Malthi left and Naveen and I returned to our prayer room. Our amazement knew no bounds that day.

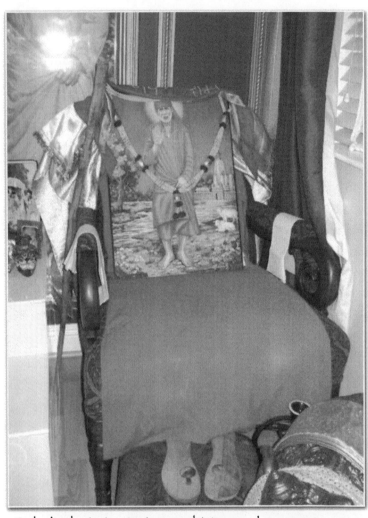

Baba's chair in Anita and Naveen's prayer room
where Malthi and Sarah saw Baba

WHATEVER YOU DO, WHEREVER YOU
MAY BE, ALWAYS BEAR THIS IN MIND:
I AM ALWAYS AWARE OF
EVERYTHING YOU DO.

Shirdi Sai Baba

CHAPTER SIX

Every Thursday we made the trip from Daly City to South San Francisco. We could not stay away. One day in the month of August during prayer, Naveen told Baba he wanted to move to South San Francisco. He wanted to be closer to Him. After bhajans the following Thursday Naveen told Malthi about his prayer. Immediately, Malthi assured him that his desire would come true.

"You will find a place in South San Francisco. It will be small in the beginning, but after a few years you will move to a larger house."

~If you seek my advice and help, it shall be given to you at once.~ Gyarah Vachan

---

We totally embraced Malthi's words and began to look for a home in South San Francisco. After all it made sense. We had begun to spend so much time with the Lal family. Holidays. Weekends. Special events. The more time we spent with the family the more I became aware that even when Shirdi Sai Baba did not totally incorporate into Malthi, she was constantly communing with Him. To be honest, I came to believe the line between Malthi's consciousness and Shirdi Sai Baba was a very thin line, if it existed at all. That belief gained credence during a trip we made as a group to the International House of Pancake (IHOP) in San Bruno, California.

Naveen and I picked up Malthi and several members of the family including Roshini. We arrived at IHOP and chose a large table that could easily accommodate Roshini's wheel chair. The breakfasts we ordered that morning included pancakes, eggs, and even fish sandwiches. While we waited for our food, Naveen was full of questions.

"Tell me Malthi, how did you find out about Baba?"

"My mom has prayed to Sathya Sai Baba for a long time; even when we lived in Fiji she prayed to Him. Then in 1992 I found out that I had brain tumor. I was paralyzed."

"You were paralyzed?" Naveen repeated, obviously stunned. Surprised as well, I simply stared at her.

"Totally paralyzed," her dark gaze emanated sincerity. "I was in a wheel chair just like Roshini."

I looked at Roshini. I tried to picture Parvati Auntie pushing two grown daughters in wheel chairs. It must have been very difficult for her physically; she is a small woman, and as a mother it could not have been anything other than an emotional abyss.

"During that time my mom constantly prayed to Baba", Malthi continued," asking Him to make me better. I was hospitalized in Stanford Hospital and my mom placed a small photo of Sathya Sai Baba in my room. I had an experience with Him."

"What kind of experience?" I asked.

"Sathya Sai Baba came out of that small picture. After He was out of the photo He grew to life size and He walked over to me. Then Baba placed His hand where I had the brain tumor. After He removed his hand He went back into the photograph. Later we found out the tumor had shrunk and I no longer needed surgery."

By now I had read several books about Sathya Sai Baba and I was not surprised by Malthi's description of how Sai Baba had come to her.

"Then what happened", Naveen asked.

"I wanted to thank Baba for helping so I went to India to see Sathya Sai Baba," Malthi replied. "I was fortunate. I actually got an interview with Him. I remember, He looked at my hands and pointed out how my fingers had four sections with three lines."

Right away I looked at my hand. "I have three sections and two lines," I reported.

"I do too," Naveen said. "Three sections and two lines. That's normal, right?"

"It is," Malthi replied, "and that is why Sathya Sai Baba said to me 'You are special.'. After He said that He did the thing he does when He's about to create something. He started circling his hand."

As Malthi explained what she experienced she imitated, with her hand, the movement Sathya Sai Baba makes. To our flabbergasted surprise vibhuti came in Malthi's hand!

Talk about shocked…I am not talking about a little bit of vibhuti. She had a hand full of vibhuti. So much vibhuti that at first she…we… didn't know what to do with it. Finally, we all took some of the sacred ash, and Malthi said, "This has never happened in a public place like a restaurant before."

Malthi was not hungry after that. I could tell she was stunned to her core. At this point in our relationship I had begun to sense that a part of Malthi simply wanted a "normal" life. She simply wanted to be a wife and a mother and have a job. Malthi wanted to share her love, which I had come to experience as a profound kind of love, with family and friends. To entertain them in a beautiful surrounding. To laugh and sing and dance. She truly wanted that and still does, but her life of miraculous occurrences was developing, and Naveen and I were graced to be a part of it.

Eventually, we all ate breakfast, but I never forgot that incident in IHOP. The data on Malthi's connection with Sai Baba was piling up in ways I never imagined possible.

Orange sindoor, tumeric and kumkum
materializing from photographs at the mandir

CHAPTER SEVEN

We found a place to live in November; a property that was literally across the street from Malthi's house. Naveen's prayers had been answered.

"Can you believe it, Naveen? Malthi's prediction has come true."

I couldn't help but think of Malthi as we carried the first item into our new home. It was a framed photo of Shiva. Naveen and I were honoring a cultural tradition to always bring the God or Goddess inside a new dwelling first. After that we carried in several more boxes and quit for the day.

The following day we continued the moving process, but inside our new home a surprise awaited us. As we rearranged some of the boxes we noticed vibhuti on the photograph of Shiva.

"Naveen look! We got vibhuti on the picture."

"Baba has blessed our house," Naveen said as he walked over to the image.

We are blessed to have Baba, I thought, *and blessed to know Malthi.*

With two children, it was difficult downsizing from four bedrooms to one bedroom. But despite the difficulty we were determined the designated dinning room would be our prayer room. There, we installed pictures of Shirdi Sai Baba, Sathya Sai Baba, and various Hindu Gods and Goddesses.

The remarkable thing about this acquisition is that the property we purchased was not for sale. With Baba's assurance we waited six months after we moved in before we actually obtained the title.

~ There shall be no want in the house of my devotees.~
Gyarah Vachan

Being close to Baba allowed us the luxury of that kind of faith, and incredible events continued to unfold in our surroundings. I also experienced powerful dreams.

There was an intriguing aspect to my dreams. Shirdi Sai Baba was my focus in my physical life, but in my dreams it was always Sathya Sai Baba who visited me. The truth is I see them as one, but I treat Shirdi Sai as God and in my dreams Sathya Sai was always my friend. The conversations Sathya Sai and I shared ranged from my inviting Him to have a coca-cola to His showing me how He manifested things.

On the night of June 16, 2001 Sathya Sai came to visit me in a dream.

"Anita," He said, "would you like to take a tour of Whitefield?"

Of course I replied, "Yes." I wanted to see His ashram in Bangalore, India. But no sooner had Baba posed the question He began to show me how He creates manifestations.

In the dream, Baba showed me his right palm. He held it up, and an interactive image of his parents, Easwaramma and Pedda Venkamma Raju, was there. Baba, who continued to sit by my side, conducted a conversation with them as I watched.

Next He showed an 'om' circling on the same palm. Sathya Sai Baba also shared with me how He manifested His physical form in other places.

"Anita," He said, "you see I am with you here."

"Yes," I replied.

"And look," He indicated the world in his hand, "I am there also."

I could see Baba inside the interactive image in his palm communing with a group of people.

Then I became aware of someone behind us who was coming to see Baba.

"I have already given them vibhuti," Baba informed me, "but I continue to sit right next to you."

What was most amazing that night was Sathya Sai Baba showed me how He incorporates into Malthi's body.

"Once again, you know I am here with you, but I am also with Malthi."

I could see Malthi inside His palm. I also saw Baba inside His palm. I watched the Baba inside His hand transform into rays of light. After Baba completely transformed Himself into rays of light He entered Malthi's body and they became one. Although Malthi and Baba were one, the next image I saw contained another Baba and Malthi inside his palm standing side by side talking.

This was the astounding manifestation process Sathya Sai Baba shared with me.

Finally, Baba took me on a tour of Whitefield in a chariot. Of all the conveyances you can think of, a chariot was the mode of transportation that He chose. I felt so fortunate traveling with Baba that night.

CHAPTER EIGHT

The number of people who attended bhajans every Thursday grew to a crowd that wavered between seventy and a hundred people. It was no longer possible for me to know everyone as I did in our early association with Malthi. One day after bhajans I overheard a short exchange between Dhiren, and a very kind looking man who showed Dhiren a pendant.

"I received this locket in a carnation last week," he said in earnest tones. "It has Sathya Sai Baba on it and I don't understand why. I am a Shirdi Sai Baba devotee. I don't believe in Sathya Sai Baba. So what does it mean?"

"Baba is letting you know both Sais are the same," Dhiren replied. "There is no difference."

The man looked down at the pendant in his hand and nodded slowly. "Thank you," he replied.

Dhiren excused himself and returned to one of the various tasks required of the Lal family. The growing Sai Family required lots of care.

As I watched Dhiren depart I felt the man was still in need of conversation, so I spoke to him. "Hello. I saw you show Dhiren your pendant."

"Yes," he replied as he showed the pendant to me. "This manifested."

I recognized and could associate with the expression on his face; a look of trying to absorb...accept what was taking place in the mandir.

"I came here for the first time last Thursday," he continued. Then he smiled, gently. "My name is Rao Pasumarthi."

"I'm Anita Bawa. Nice to meet you."

"Nice to meet you," he said. "Have you been coming here for long?"

"It's been about one year," I replied. "And I've seen some amazing things take place during that time."

"No doubt," his fine boned face lit up. "I got this last week and I couldn't believe it. I took the carnation Baba gave me when He came and I put the flower in my pocket. I didn't look at it any more until I got home. That's when I saw the locket."

"Very nice," I said; glad for him. "How did you find out about the mandir?

"I was looking for a good place for me to go for bhajans," Rao explained. "I started believing in Shirdi Sai Baba when I was still in India, but I never believed in Sathya Sai Baba. When I was a little boy around ten years old my mother would take me to where Sathya Sai Baba was, but it was basically for the *prasad*." He shook his head. "There was no belief. Then I came to the United States and I started living in Florida. For awhile I attended bhajans in Florida with some Sathya Sai Baba devotees." Rao drew a calming breath. "And eventually I made a move to California, and I wanted to attend bhajans again. A friend of mine told me about this place, and he showed me a Ganesh *murti* that he received from the shrine here. I was totally baffled by what he said about it. I didn't understand how this could happen. You see I'm a microbiologist...a scientist.

Nothing can be created or destroyed. Then this happened to me." He looked at the pendant then looked back at me. "All I can say is what is happening here is super natural."

This was the kind of reception many people received at the South San Francisco mandir. They would come, and they would experience one or more of the constant flow of miracles. After that I deduced one of three things occurred. Those people would either return because they believed what they experienced; return because they didn't quite believe but found it all very entertaining, or they did not return because they did not believe it.

By far the majority of the people who came to Malthi's mandir were Hindus, although Sai Baba taught acceptance of all religions. His wide-ranged philosophy opened my life to the concept of God as one no matter the religion. The Lal family wanted to share Baba's inclusive viewpoint with everyone, and one evening Sarita arrived at bhajans with an image of Jesus she had removed from a calendar and framed. Sarita said Parvati Auntie wanted to include a representation of Jesus on their altar, and because Sarita felt close to Jesus Parvati Auntie asked her to provide it.

The image of Jesus was placed on the altar with other objects of worship which included a weekly offering of a glass of water. In no less than one week vibhuti appeared in Jesus' heart. But what would be considered by some as even more remarkable, because of the biblical connection, was little by little that water turned to red wine.

Manifestations were a constant in the mandir. For me some of them were more compelling than others. One evening as I sat in my regular spot against the wall and Sarita sat further in the rear of the prayer room, Baba motioned Sarita forward for an honor that had become a regular part of bhajans. It involved a large, silver colored bowl that was kept near Baba's chair.

As customary, Sarita knelt in front of Baba and slid the bowl toward His feet. He placed His feet in the bowl and Sarita poured water on His feet before she gently washed them. After she completed her task Sarita patted Baba's feet dry and the bowl was removed. It was a privilege that was performed on many occasions, and the person performing the task was the first person to receive Baba's blessing.

That evening Sarita continued to kneel, waiting for whatever form Baba's blessing would take. It was a normal scene in the mandir; a person kneeling in front of Baba who sat quietly. Normal that is…until slowly, but surely, Baba's body began to move as if He needed to regurgitate. Baba continued that motion for perhaps two minutes and during that time He appeared to be experiencing definite discomfort. Then in the midst of His body going through this wave, Shirdi Sai Baba pointed behind Him to a Krishna statue and after that He opened His mouth and gagged. Baba gagged several times before a small *murti* came out of His mouth. It was a tiny, metal statue of Krishna. Baba gave that statue to Sarita.

It's astonishing that a statue would come out of Baba's body, but even beyond that is… Baba indicated who, what God, would emerge from His body before it emerged. Later I found out from Sarita that the blessing of the Krishna statue held the deepest of meanings for her, for it has always been Krishna who has been embedded in her heart.

Jesus image materializing vibhuti with
the water turned to wine

CHAPTER NINE

Our lives with Malthi as a friend were quite ordinary outside of bhajans, as ordinary as that could possibly be. I recall one day in July Malthi and I decided to start walking as part of a new exercise routine.

On our first walking day we were headed out of the door when Naveen said, "Can I join you guys?"

"Sure, why not," I said.

"Bhayia," Malthi added enthusiastically, "yes, you can join us."

After that the three of us began the walk together.

We headed in the direction of Orange Park. The conversation was pleasantly light and general. Exercise was on the brain and nothing else until Malthi passed a branch of a tree and it hit the side of her face.

"Something happened," she said in a somewhat peculiar fashion.

I looked at her but I had no idea what she was talking about.

"What happened?" Naveen asked.

"Do you know who is walking with you?" Malthi began, "What would you do if I disappeared?"

Naveen looked at Malthi intently. "Is Baba walking with us?"

"Maybe," was the solitary reply.

I simply didn't understand their strange conversation. I could not grasp the possibility that Baba had popped in to walk with us. So we continued our walk, and when we were done Malthi returned with us to our house. As soon as she entered our home Malthi took a seat in the living room.

"Naveen," Malthi said his name with a somewhat official flair, "Baba is here. Please perform the **aarthi**." Through those simple words Malthi acknowledged Baba had come during our walk. Baba had joined us in Orange Park.

I prepared the aarthi with ghee and a single wick. By now we had experienced so much through Malthi I did not question her instructions when it came to Baba. When the aarthi was ready I handed it to Naveen and he lit the wick and offered the flame to Baba... Malthi.

Because the flame was sacred, after Naveen performed the aarthi I couldn't simply put it out, so I went to our prayer room to allow it to burn out naturally. What did I see when I arrived there? I saw fresh sprinkles of vibhuti on many of the pictures of the Gods and Goddesses. It was proof that Baba had come and blessed us and our home once again.

~If you look to me, I look to you.~ Gyarah Vachan

Our lives continued to flow in a positive direction because of Baba. One aspect of that was we were able to make structural changes to our new home. Our current house was definitely small for our family, as Baba said it would be, so we built two bedrooms downstairs. By the time the dust settled on the renovations preparations for Naveen's 40th birthday celebration were in full swing, and somewhere along the way the event turned into a Sai event. We invited our entire Sai family along with other family members. This meant bhajans were held in our home for the first time. It was such an honor; one that Naveen and I didn't take lightly.

At the end of bhajans all of the attendees headed downstairs where food and drinks were being served. But in light of it being Naveen's birthday celebration I stayed behind with my mom, Simla Bawa, and Naveen. She wanted to bless Naveen.

I watched my mother take a pinch of orange **sindoor**. Afterwards she placed it on Naveen's forehead.

"I am blessing you for good health and prosperity, Naveen. God always be with you," and to my surprise she closed her eyes, and added, "Baba, I would love to feel your presence here tonight."

I knew my mom included that last sentence in her blessing because she had heard Naveen and I talk about the Baba miracles we witnessed in our home and at the South San Francisco mandir. Constantly we shared those amazing events with family members because we were compelled to share them with the ones we loved.

After my mom blessed Naveen she turned and looked at a large Sathya Sai Baba photo that hung a few feet away.

"Look! Look. Vibhuti is coming!" Her voice quivered with excitement as she watched orange sindoor come out of the photograph. "I am so happy Baba is blessing you," my mother declared.

There was a rush of excitement downstairs as everyone returned to the prayer room when they heard my mother's voice. The proof of Baba's blessing was plain for all to see in the form of a large splash of orange sindoor. Acknowledgments and conversations erupted all around over the grace that we witnessed. To this very day that sindoor continues to come out of that Sathya Sai Baba photograph in our prayer room.

It took a while before the excitement over Baba's miracle waned. When it did, we continued to celebrate Naveen's birthday with food, music, dance and with the knowledge that Baba celebrated with us.

Orange sindoor started manifesting when Anita's mother asked Baba to make His presence felt during Naveen's birthday celebration

CHAPTER TEN

The following Thursday Ashu was in exceptionally high spirits.

"Did you hear what happened last week?" He smiled broadly. "It was a misri day."

"A misri day???" I had no idea what he meant by that. "What happened, Ashu?" I asked, very curious.

"You know Amma is always making those long garlands for Sathya Sai Baba's photo, right?"

Ashu called Malthi's mother Amma because Baba told him he and Malthi had been sister and brother in a previous life. "Yes, I know she does," I replied.

"Have you seen her shake it? And seen all the misri that falls out of the garland?" He continued to tease the moment.

I shook my head. "No, I have never seen Parvati Auntie do that."

"Well, she does after the puja," Ashu informed me, "and the little pieces of sugar candy fall from the garland and end up on the floor."

I giggled. "With Baba anything is possible."

"It definitely is." Ashu smiled again. "You've got to hear

this. Baba can be so many things. Okay." He inhaled deeply. "Before bhajans today, Amma asked me and Justin to clean the mandir. So we came to the puja room and dusted and cleaned and picked up any stray pieces of misri from the floor. Well...I thought we had totally cleaned the room when I looked on the floor and there were a few more pieces of candy. I asked Justin, 'Why did you leave those pieces of misri?' Justin told me he had cleaned that side but I didn't believe him, so I went and picked up all the candy I saw. By the time we were preparing to go back downstairs there was more misri on the floor, so we knew it was Baba playing a game with us."

I was totally amused by Ashu's story. I never thought of Baba in such a playful way. Bhajans. Sindoor and murti manifestions. Prayers. I related those things to Baba. But a game for the sake of fun? Never.

'After we picked up all the misri on the floor we went downstairs," Ashu continued, "But Justin wanted to go back into the puja room by himself so he could get more misri if Baba had materialized it. I wasn't having that." Ashu chuckled. "I told him we started this together and we would end it together. So we returned to the puja room and there were three pieces of misri on the side of the room I had just cleaned, three pieces on the side Justin cleaned, and one in the center. Baba had turned it into a competition and we raced to get the middle piece." Ashu laughed. "We had so much fun with Baba that day. He put misri on a water gun Justin had played with; he put a big piece next to my car that was parked outside, and one inside of Justin's shirt. That day we collected about one hundred pieces of misri. It was definitely a sweet day."

"It was, wasn't it," I said.

Ashu nodded. "When I told this to Amma she said, "Every

time you go into the mandir there is always some kind of miracle."

I believe that is true. I'm certain Parvati Auntie could make such a claim because through the years she experienced much more than I did. Many attendees experienced Baba's miracles. There was a steady flow of people who came to Shree Shirdi Sai Baba of South San Francisco with their ailments and troubles on Thursdays and inevitably in a couple of weeks returned to report how they had been cured or their problem had been solved. I am certain the tangible results people received were the driving force behind the growing number of attendees. They did not appear to be reluctant to lay their burdens on Baba in His South San Francisco form. I guess that is because when human beings are in pain we simply want results.

Once Rao asked Malthi, "What do you experience when Baba comes?"

"What I can say is this," she replied. "When I am deeply concentrating on Baba in bhajans I begin to hear lots of bells ringing. Then there's a kind of smoke that comes, and I feel something like a jolt of energy...a shock. After that I don't recall anything because Baba has come."

Ganesh materializing misri in the mandir: 2002

IF WE SEE ALL ACTIONS AS GOD'S
DOING, WE WILL BE UNATTACHED
AND FREE FROM KARMIC BONDAGE.

Shirdi Sai Baba

CHAPTER ELEVEN

With little fanfare Baba continued to show His ability to create. One evening during bhajans in 2002 Baba drew what appeared to be imaginary figures near the floor. Afterwards He selected five devotees, Naveen was one of them. He instructed them to go and see what was on the deck.. When they stepped onto the structure which was adjacent to the bhajan hall; they were dumbstruck by what they saw. A complete *dhuni* was there accompanied by Baba's large handprint. Before He left Baba instructed Malthi to light the sacred fire within it. There were do many things…we could never guess what Baba would do.

During this period of my life I continued to experience many dreams with Sathya Sai Baba. The dreams were prolific and felt extremely real. They ranged from Baba visiting bhajans I attended; visiting my home and advising me about my health and family; to a visit with Baba in Puttaparthi, India where Sathya Sai's Prashanti Nilayam ashram is located . Because of the relationship I developed with Sathya Sai Baba during these night visits I decided to go to India to see Sathya Sai Baba in February 2002.

I started making plans in January. I secured an airplane ticket, visas, and an itinerary that included Singapore, but through a freak fall I suffered a terrible break in the form of a protruding bone from the upper portion of my left arm. I had to cancel my plans. Needless to say I was extremely disappointed, and I wondered why Baba didn't want me to come to India. I was burdened by the thought of it until He told me why in a dream.

"Why do you want to come to me when I come to you," Sathya Sai Baba said before he added, "Why Fear When I am Here?"

"But Baba, I want to see you in your physical form at least one time in my life, although I know you do come to me," I replied.

"Yes, you will come to me one day. But for now please take care of the tenderness in your arm."

For a year I took care of myself and my arm, and finally I journeyed to India with some of my Sai Family in February, 2003. Our first destination was Shirdi. Naveen and I took a train there. On that train we encountered a man who strongly emanated the energy of Shirdi Sai Baba, and he physically reminded us of Him. The man's clothes were tattered; his hair and beard were white and he sat and held his head like Baba. I offered him money and he refused the money, but he said he would accept food. Naveen and I bought some food from a train vendor; gave it to the man and touched his feet before we took leave of him. After that he got off at the next stop. Anyone who has ridden a train in India knows it can be grueling, but after 'the Baba" left our sitting arrangement and everything improved immensely.

I must confess my memories of my first time in Shirdi, India are rather vague. The truth is I traveled to India because of Sathya Sai Baba's visits in my dreams. At the time Shirdi was not that important to me because we had Shirdi Sai Baba in South San Francisco. After Shirdi we traveled to Puttaparthi where several of my family members joined us; while Malthi and other devotees headed to Bangalore. Puttaparthi was the place where I was confronted with the reality that some dreams are not just dreams. When we arrived at Prashanti Nilayam, Sathya Sai Baba's ashram, I recognized the gate!

"Naveen, remember my dream where Baba gave me the tour of His ashram? This is exactly the gate that I saw in my dream."

I knew I had never researched anything on Sathya Sai Baba or His ashrams. To see the truth of what I had "dreamed" as a physical reality was astonishing. Yet, by now nothing seemed to surprise Naveen after all we had witnessed in South San Francisco but that didn't curtail my enthusiasm. Naveen had to bear my exclamations of delight each time I announced I had seen this or that structure during my night time visit with Sathya Sai Baba. From the Chaitanya Jyoti Museum, to the replica of Krishna's chariot, I recognized many things in Puttaparthi. We stayed in that city for five days. While we were there we crossed paths with Malthi and several other Sai members. It was great to spend some time with them.

Vaishno Devi temple in Jammu and Kashmir State was next on all of our itineraries, but once again Naveen and I had different travel arrangements from Malthi's group, so we separated and headed north more than a thousand miles.

The climb to see Vaishno Devi is known to be a tough climb. Naveen and I were ready to bear it but amazingly enough we were graced with the use of six military horses and three guards to escort us up the Trikuta Mountain; courtesy of my brother-in-law, Sunil Goswami, who is a General Major in the Indian Army. We experienced Mata's darshan three times that day. It was an exceptional twenty-four hours.

When we returned to South San Francisco I discovered Malthi climbed the fourteen snow covered kilometers in her bare feet! I had no idea what motivated her to seek Vaishno Devi in such a pious way. Who is it besides Baba who knows the purpose of his *lila*s, and believe me there was a significant purpose behind Malthi's trip.

Later I was told Malthi had a dream when she returned to California. Vaishno Devi appeared to her and requested that Malthi return to India right away. The Goddess said if Malthi did not return to her, Vaishno Devi promised she would come to Malthi. I assume Malthi felt she had done all she could or wanted to do, and she decided not to return to India despite Mata's request. At the time I knew nothing about Malthi's dream.

Baba continued to give darshan sporadically during the next month. One night after Baba gave darshan Malthi was recuperating as she always did because of the strenuous physical demands the longer incorporations required of her body. You see, at this point in Malthi's relationship with Baba, she doesn't know what transpires while Baba is there. She does not remember the materializations or conversations. It is quite a process to behold, and when Baba comes His energy is so powerful the weight of Malthi's female body increases tremendously.

Well, while Malthi was recuperating this particular evening Dhiren made an announcement that surprised the Sai family and Malthi.

"Baba wants all of you to know that He will not be giving darshan for the next year. Malthi is going to be a mother."

Immediately I looked at Malthi. There was a combination of joy and confusion on her face. It was obvious Malthi was happy over the announcement, but it also looked as if she wondered how this great feat was going to be accomplished. I knew Malthi wanted more children. She had expressed that over the years, but her desire for more children had proven to be easier said than done because Malthi's medical history was a huge hurdle, and at the point and time of the announcement we knew Malthi was not expecting.

I've got to say I was totally surprised by this new development. Baba had been giving darshan approximately every three weeks or so for the last year, so to hear he would not be giving darshan for more than a year because Malthi was having a baby amazed me. Actually I had mixed feelings about it. I was happy for Malthi but I was sad that we would not get to see Baba for almost a year.

From the looks on the collective faces of the close Sai Family; we were all astounded. Some of the men like Rao and Bakul Patel appeared surprised but were taking the announcement in stride. Sarita stared at Malthi while Geeti Jayasurya looked extremely happy laced with elements of surprise, but it was Malthi's mother, Parvati Aunties joy that was most apparent.

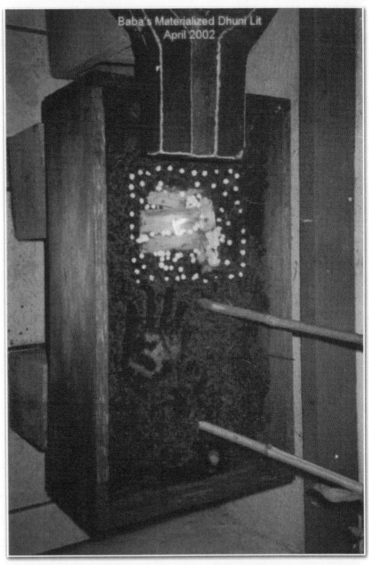

Lit dhuni materialized by Baba: 2002

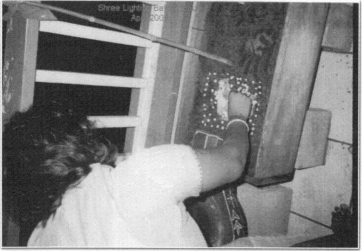

Materialized dhuni with Baba's handprint with
Malthi lighting it: 2002

CHAPTER TWELVE

Baba's words are as good as gold. I experienced the power of his foretelling the future over and over again, and I totally trusted what Baba said. In 2003, the large home Baba promised Naveen and I would be part of our lives was well on its way. Being so close to Baba and Malthi was a marvel in our lives. We wanted to show our gratitude by celebrating Shirdi Sai Baba's upcoming birthday in our brand new prayer room. In order to do so, because our house was still under construction we requested of all the rooms in our house, that the construction company complete our prayer room first. As a result they insured us the prayer room would be ready by September 28th. In other words, a bare-boned constructed prayer room would be ready for transformation into a place worthy of the festivity. This meant the night before Baba's birthday celebration was extremely hectic.

"What we need to do is focus on framing the posters," Naveen said as I put my energy into what I felt was important. "We do not need to worry about carpet or painting the room. I want the frames for Baba's posters to be painted and put together before tomorrow morning."

"Yes, I know you want these frames to be completed but we also need to set up the room for the ceremony," I stressed.

We were both tired and somewhat frazzled but we continued to do what we thought was necessary. Naveen busied himself with framing two life size posters; one of Sathya Sai Baba and one of Shirdi Sai Baba. We wanted those posters to be the focus of our prayer room. Work continued deep into the night, and it was about 1 a.m. in the morning when Naveen finished the framing. We grabbed what sleep we could after that; got up in the morning and continued the preparations. By the time the gathering started I was exhausted, but we were ready.

Malthi conducted the prayer. There were perhaps twenty of us. The group included the Lal family, Ashu, Sarita and Geeti. Before the ceremony I must confess I was concerned about the safety of my guests. Literally, they had to walk through a construction site in order to enter the prayer room, but once the bhajans began I was relieved and grateful that it had come together so nicely. As I watched Malthi close the ceremony by performing the *aarthi*, I knew Baba had arranged it all. We could not have pulled it off without His blessing, and prasad in the form of fruit was served before we left the room.

Everyone was interested in how the construction of the house was progressing, so Naveen and I gave a tour. We walked the framed-out rooms with nails, sawdust and small pieces of wood scattered on the concrete floors. In the midst of this Malthi said, "You are blessed. Once again Baba has blessed your house. Go see your prayer room."

Excited, we returned to the room. Immediately my gaze focused on a large clump of vibhuti on the life size image of Shirdi Sai Baba. The manifestation of His blessing was there. It seemed no matter how many times Baba proved to us that He knew what was happening in our daily lives, the level of joy

I received from that proof never lessened. It was proof that God existed, and we knew we were extremely blessed to have such personal experiences with Him.

After all of the Sai family witnessed that Baba had made his presence known, we left the prayer room to enjoy lunch in our old living room located across the yard.

As you most likely can tell from this account by this time our lives were inseparable from Malthi's family. Now when I look back I have no doubt that Baba forged this relationship because He knows the past, present and future, and it is obvious to me that the close relationship was a part of our karmic destiny. Because of that relationship when we moved into our completed new home Naveen and I felt as if it was also the Lal family's home; and I became aware of an interesting theme that began to emerge.

First, Malthi became pregnant as Baba foretold, but that was only the tip of the iceberg. That pregnancy was the most unusual pregnancy I have ever witnessed. During the entire pregnancy Malthi could not eat food or keep it down. Nothing. So what did they do during this extremely challenging time? Intravenous feeding for the entire second trimester. Malthi was so weak that she could not walk or even go to the bathroom without assistance. She also had to take blood clot preventing injections daily. Can you imagine the resolve it must have taken to see this unusual pregnancy to its fulfillment? Or the care that was needed to help Malthi see it through? I deeply admire Malthi's mom, Parvati Auntie, who looked after her every minute as she juggled the others issues that arose in their lives.

"You do so much for everyone," I said to her one day. "Cooking, cleaning, preparing and praying for the puja on Thursday, and taking care of Malthi during this time. But you also have Roshini to care for, and now that Ram Lal Uncle is in the hospital you visit him everyday." I marveled at her strength, tenacity and dedication.

"Baba tests us so much," Parvati replied, "but he blesses us too in special ways." Her eyes lit up. "We have been told the baby who is coming is Vaishnavi."

Now…I had a feeling from all that was occurring around the pregnancy that this had to be a special child. After all Malthi is a special person. She had climbed fourteen kilometers barefooted in the snow as a prayer to Vaishnavi in India, and as the Goddess foretold when Malthi did not return to India after her trip, Vaishnavi had come to her.

Vibhuti manifestation in Anita and Naveen's prayer room

CHAPTER THIRTEEN

Baba's birthday celebration came, and He bestowed on all who attended the same amazing generosity He always gave. Various murtis and jewelry were given to many. Baba's kindness permeated the mandir and our hearts when He gave personal darshan to everyone. He answered our questions and calmed our fears. But you can not imagine one of the greatest gifts of all. That gift is to see Baba dance! To see Him take His walking stick and move rhythmically with His shoulders hunched, His back rounded. That is pure joy.

Opportunity for blessings continued to pour into our home. First we hosted Malthi's baby shower which was lots of fun, and no more than thirty days later we held an official house warming with Sai bhajans. All of our friends and relatives brought presents for the house and we were very grateful. Ashu brought a special gift; a beautiful statue of Shirdi Baba. It was on that statue that Baba blessed us with vibhuti during our house warming.

A few weeks later, on December 22nd, a baby girl named Shruthi was born. Her birth was accompanied by the Sai family's joy that an aspect of Vaishnavi had joined us.

Life is such an unending play of which Baba knows the twist and turns. We are simply actors on the stage of life, hopefully playing our roles to the best of our abilities. There is an old saying about the opening and closing of doors in life. That is how I felt during that time. You see, Ram Lal uncle's sickness was a constant during that period. When he passed away in January, 2004 there was an onslaught of sadness, and as a result of Hindu tradition, the Lal family decided not have any family celebrations for a year, but bhajans continued on Thursdays. I knew Malthi was extremely sad about his transition. She was very close to her father. He was a man who occupied a special place in the hearts of his physical family and many Sai family members; a man who enjoyed his physical life and understood the value of a rich spiritual one.

No matter the depths of the spiritual existence that Malthi lived, how her life appeared to be a life of blessings and admiration; I had come to know it was much more complicated than that. Outside of the physical karma…the illnesses that she took from others into her body so they would not suffer but she did, I believe knowing things before anyone else knew…things that were deeply personal and painful, was not easy. That was the case when it came to Malthi and her father. Years before his time came Malthi told some of us that her father would get lung cancer, how long he would suffer with the disease and when he would part. She was accurate on all accounts. But amazing enough Malthi also knew it would only be a short time before her father would begin his next life and where that new life would start.

Once Parvati Auntie was asked why Baba came into her daughter in such a powerful way but at the same time seemed to allow her such suffering.

"Baba said before Malthi entered into this life, before she

was born," Parvati began, "she vowed by writing with her own blood that she would help alleviate sickness and suffering. She vowed to take it on herself. Malthi literally wrote it down while she lived in the *loka* from which she came," Parvati spoke rapidly, clearly. "Once someone makes a vow like that it is very strong, Baba says. Only Baba can lessen it, but even that would take time, because it was Malthi's right to make such a vow. But to make a vow there and then to live it here is two different things. Still, Malthi takes on the diseases out of her love for the devotees who come here. She barely sleeps at night because she is constantly praying for someone. When Malthi does sleep the prayers continue. I have seen her hands form sacred mudras as she sleeps." Parvati's expression turned into one of surrender. "I do not know the how and why of Baba's lilas, but I have seen the proof that they exist through my daughter's life."

CHAPTER FOURTEEN

Three months after Malthi gave birth to Shruti, Baba returned to giving darshan. For me it felt like an eternity, and we were all very happy to see Baba again.

One evening when Naveen and I were relaxing at home watching TV Asia, we saw Narendra Chanchal ji, a well known Indian devotional singer, was scheduled to perform Mata songs in Hindu temples in the United States. They also advertised if anyone else was interested in Narendra Chanchal ji performing in their home, they could contact his representative via a telephone number that ran across the bottom of our television screen.

"Since Narendra Chanchal ji is coming to the States, do you want him to come to our house to perform Mata's Chowki." Naveen asked.

My first reaction was to say, "No," but when they gave the phone number a second time I wrote it down.

"So many amazing prayers have been answered in our home," Naveen said. "It will be good to have him in our new home to perform Mata's songs. Malthi has said you have Mata energy", Naveen teased, "if you do have Mata's energy you can get Narendra Chanchal ji to come for our event."

Although Naveen's comment about Malthi making an association between me and Mata was challenging; the truth is I don't know why I wrote down the number because I was definitely on the fence when it came to Naveen's idea. Still my hesitancy did not deter my husband, who continued to challenge my ability to arrange a performance in our home by Narendra Chanchal ji; and because Naveen knows me well, in short order I took the bait. I picked up the telephone and dialed the number.

"TV Asia," a professional voice announced through the phone.

"I would like to schedule Narendra Chanchal's Mata's Chowki on Tuesday, July 22nd," I said, looking at Naveen. "Is this date available?"

"Let me check the calendar," the female voice replied, "Hold please."

Silence filled the line as I waited.

In short order the representative returned to the telephone and said, "Can I take your name and number? We will call you back about the availability of this date."

I gave the information she requested and hung up. The following day I received a call from a TV Asia representative. She advised us the date was available, and then confirmed our house was now on Narendra Chanchal's schedule. I was absolutely amazed.

Talk about preparation. It took us three weeks to prepare for this event. Early on the appointed day we welcomed Narendra Chanchal ji, his wife, his sponsor, Bhalla, his wife and their children into our home. Introductions were made and soon after we invited them into our prayer room.

Moments after Bhalla entered the room he posed a question. "What is on the pictures?" He pointed. "The red, orange and gray powders?"

With all the preparations we made I hadn't prepared for answering questions about Baba's materializations.

"It is sindoor," I replied, "different color vibhut's that Baba materialized for us."

"Really?" He replied.

I got the feeling Bhalla didn't quite believe my explanation.

To my relief, and before Naveen or I could say more, Narendra Chanchal ji gave a reply.

"I have seen these miracles, Bhalla," he said. "It's God's grace. Take it at face value."

From Bhalla's response it appeared that's exactly what he did. Nothing more was said. They left our home and returned to the house later that evening before the event.

There were more than 200 people waiting for the performance, including Malthi and our Sai family. In order to accommodate the crowd, we emptied out the entire bottom floor of our three storied home. We set up the stage for Narendra Chanchal ji to perform in our living room, while catered food was kept warm for our guests in a large, white tent outside. Many people were able to enjoy dinner before the performance began.

Narendra Chanchal ji opened his performance with a Shirdi Baba bhajan, and then sang continuously for more than three hours. It was an exquisite performance, and it was obvious everyone who attended enjoyed themselves immensely.

Before he left the stage and returned to the private room we had designated for him upstairs, Narendra Chanchal ji said, "Naveen and his family were already blessed with Baba, and now they are also blessed with Mata's presence."

Once again food was partaken and slowly the crowd dwindled to a hand full of us who wanted to take pictures with Narendra Chanchal ji. Naveen was the coordinator of that much desired part of the evening, and photographs were taken in a private room which was across from our closed prayer room.

After such a powerful performance I felt drawn to the prayer room; so I opened the door and went inside. There, on a modest statue of Durga Mata, was a mound of red kumkum… red sindoor. I felt blessed to be the first one to see it, and I went to find Bhalla.

"Come with me," I said when I reached him.

Bhalla obeyed my request and followed me to our prayer room.

Once inside I pointed to Durga Mata's kumkum. "Look," I directed Bhalla's attention, "this was not here when you came earlier today."

I remember the look on his face to this day. It was priceless.

"Wow," was Bhalla's response.

This time, I knew he believed me.

The following morning we had the pleasure of hosting Narendra Chanchal ji and his entourage for breakfast. After breakfast Narendra Chanchal ji turned to me and asked, "May I have some of the sindoor and some of Baba's vibhuti from your prayer room?"

Bhalla joined in on the request.

"Sure. Why not?" I replied."

I went upstairs and made several packets of kumkum and vibhuti to give to them. It had been a wonderful event; one that I may experience only once in this lifetime, and I was grateful to Baba and Mata for showing their presence that day.

Kumkum that manifested during Narendra
Chanchal ji's performance

CHAPTER FIFTEEN

Sara, my ten years old daughter, developed a strong desire to go to India to see Sathya Sai Baba. So when my sabbatical time arrived, Sara, my sister, Rita, and I packed our bags and went on a multiple country tour that culminated in India.

~ Whoever puts his feet on Shirdi soil his suffering would come to an end. ~ Gyarah Vachan

Shirdi, for me, now is the most special place in the world. There are no words to explain it, and I do not doubt that I lived in Shirdi, India before.

~ The wretched and miserable would rise into plenty of joy and happiness, as soon as they climb the steps of my Samadhi. ~ Gyarah Vachan

When I am there I know I am home, and perhaps, in some way, because of that original connection Baba has seen it fit for me to live this lifetime in the Shirdi of the western world, South San Francisco. Baba has proclaimed many times that the Shirdi in India and the Shirdi in South San Francisco are energetically the same. His Samadhi is in India but because He comes to South San Francisco, the Gyarah Vashan, His eleven sayings, are also fulfilled in California.

When we were in Shirdi in 2004, there was one special person there who dressed liked Baba, looked like Baba, and spoke like Baba. I saw this man everywhere during my stay in Shirdi. If I went to Dwarkamai, he was standing outside the door... if I went to the Neem tree, he was there...if I went to the main mandir he was also there. Needless to say I became very curious, *Who is this man?* I thought, and that launched my search into the streets of Shirdi to learn more about him. Eventually I found him. It was at midnight of August the 15th. He was sitting beneath a small tree. I went up to him and touched his feet.

He blessed me by touching my head. "Do not rush to get things done," he said, "especially when you are eating."

Those were the first words out of his mouth and I could not believe it. A couple of hours earlier I rushed by brother-in-law to eat faster because I wanted to go. I wanted to go to find this man. How did he know that?

"Are you Shirdi Baba?" I asked.

He gave a slight smile.

"Do you live in Shirdi?" I attempted to find out more about him.

"I live half of the time here in Shirdi and half of my time in the Himalayas," he replied

"Can I get you anything to eat?" I asked.

"No, I already ate. I only eat one meal a day." He pointed at a black dog. "You can give milk to the dog."

Before I left I acquired milk for the dog and fed him.

The following day Sara, Rita and Bhupinder Giri, my brother-in-law, and I went to the Samadhi mandir.

When we arrived professional singers were performing Baba's bhajans perhaps two hundred feet away from Baba's Samadhi. Quietly, we joined in and took a seat beside them. We sang for at least two hours. During that time Sara sang a solo bhajan – Bolo Bolo Sub Milo Bolo Om Namah Shivaya.

Once Sara's bhajan was done we saw "that Baba" enter the mandir. He walked toward the stage and approached Sara. I watched as he removed his necklace and handed it to my daughter. It was a chain with a locket featuring Shirdi Sai on one side and Shiva on the other. Then he produced a key chain from his pocket that was decorated with Laxmi Mata.

"Here," he said, "give this to your mother."

"Thank you," Sara replied. With those parting actions and words "Baba" turned and walked away.

*~My tomb shall bless and speak to the needs
of my devotees.~* Gyarah Vachan

CHAPTER SIXTEEN

That week in Shirdi remains close to my heart. Puttaparthi was a different experience.

In order to experience the darshan of Sathya Sai Baba we managed to navigate the strict discipline that is adhered to inside Prashanti Nilayam. Sara found a special treat in there; the western canteen. She enjoyed the ashram canteen immensely because some of her favorite western foods were available.

There was one significant conversation that occurred in Prashanti Nilayam. I read a notice that announced Anil Kumar, the main translator for Sathya Sai Baba, was holding satsang. We decided to attend. In no time at all we found the building and entered the small room where the event was being held. The four of us sat and listened as Mr. Kumar told old stories about Sathya Sai Baba's life.

When his talk was done he addressed the audience.

"Anyone have questions that they would like to ask me?"

Out of the group of about ten people a few posed questions, including my sister. I sat quietly during the exchange. Then I had a question of my own.

"Are Baba's dreams just dreams, or does Baba actually come in dreams?"

"Baba's dreams are not dreams. They are visions of Baba. Do not say dreams," Anil Kumar continued. "They are Baba's visions, and He actually comes to deliver a message to you."

I felt a kind of elation hearing this, because over the past four years I had many visions of Baba during the night.

Later that day another special event occurred. It began when Buphinder introduced us to a man named Husmukh.

"He is from Geneva, Switzerland," Buphinder said as motioned toward the thin, blond man, "and he knows a woman who knew Shirdi Sai Baba. He is willing to take us to see her. She is 105 years old now. Her name is Mrs. V. Bala Tripura Sundari."

"She lives right here in the ashram," Husmukh informed us. "I do not know if you have heard of her but she is known throughout the Sai community for how she came to accept that Sathya Sai and Shirdi Sai Baba are the same. Mrs. Sundari's husband was a Shirdi Sai devotee, and she had her first darshan of Baba in Shirdi when she was thirteen years old. Shirdi Sai Baba gave her a Shivalingam in a silver case and padukas. Back in the 50's she ended up living in Prashanti Nilyam, but she always wanted to return to Shirdi because Mrs. Sundari considered Shirdi Sai Baba as her Baba, not Sathya Sai. Then one day Sathya Sai Baba came to her and said 'It seems you don't want to stay here.' And she hesitantly told Him she wanted to go to Shirdi. He asked her what would she find in Shirdi when He was in Prashanti, and Sathya Sai Baba told her one day Puttaparthi would be a big city and that she would see it. Well...Mrs. Sundari ended up blurting out that her Baba was in Shirdi and the next thing she knew Baba said, 'Look!' And right in front of her He disappeared and

Shirdi Sai Baba was there. She was so overwhelmed she fell at his feet. When Mrs. Sundari looked up again He was Sathya Sai Baba. After that he teased if she was still leaving and of course she said no." Husmukh cleared his throat. "At some point later on Baba asked Mrs. Sundari to give back to Him the Shivalingam He gave her. She didn't know what Sathya Sai Baba was talking about, and she told Him He never gave her a Shivalingam. That's when Sathya Sai Baba recounted the whole incident of how He gave her the Shivalingam, the silver cover and the padukas when He was Shirdi Sai Baba. He told her she could keep the padukas and the silver cover but He wanted the Shivalingam. Mrs. Sundari said when she gave him the Shivalingam He removed it from the case and gave the case to her; and as He held the Shivalingam in His hand it simply disappeared. Mrs. Sundari still has the padukas, but she gave the silver case that held the Shivalingam back to Baba many years ago."

After hearing that of course I wanted to meet the woman who experienced such a rich validation of Shirdi Sai and Sathya Sai being the same Being.

We followed Husmukh to East Prashanti, a building that is right beside the main platform where Sathya Sai Baba gives darshan. After we mounted the stairs to the 2nd floor; we knocked on one of the doors and a middle aged woman greeted us.

"Sai Ram," she said as she invited us to come in. "Would you care for a glass of water or tea?"

Respectfully, we declined the offer. I looked out the window and noticed anyone inside could have a clear view of Sathya Sai Baba whenever He gave darshan.

"Would you like to see the padukas that Shirdi Baba gave to my great mother-in-law when he was still alive in Shirdi?

"Yes," we all said.

She guided us toward a small altar in another room. The padukas were kept in a special place in the middle of other sacred statues and photographs. We honored the small silver sandals by gently touching them before we placed our finger tips to our foreheads. Mrs. Sundari, who received the padukas from Shirdi Sai Baba, was resting quietly in a chair in another room. Before we left, we also honored her by touching her feet.

On our way to the airport in a rental car profusely decorated with marigolds, I recalled Baba saying, "Why do you want to come to India to see me when I come to you in South San Francisco?" I felt as if He was giving me a royal send off saying, now you have come. Go home. I am there.

WHY FEAR WHEN I AM HERE?

Shirdi Sai Baba

CHAPTER SEVENTEEN

Because Malthi's family was in the midst of honoring the Hindu tradition associated with her father's transition, Shridi Sai Baba's birthday was celebrated at the home of another Sai family in Hayward, California. Our home was chosen for Sathya Sai Baba's birthday festivities.

The night before the celebration, once again, we emptied the main floor to prepare. Dhiren came up with the idea of erecting an altar in our living room decorated with colorful saris. What he created could only have been accomplished with Baba's grace, because when he was finished we all stood back and admired the transformation.

"Very nice, "I said as I took in the various shades of red with sparkling accents.

"It is good," Naveen concurred.

"I like it too," Malthi agreed. "Now we should bring down Sathya Sai Baba's pictures from the prayer room."

"Which pictures?" Naveen asked.

"Any of them," Malthi replied.

That portion of the preparations appeared to be under control so I asked as Naveen started up the stairs, "Does anyone want a cup of tea?"

"Yes," they replied unanimously.

I started making tea and Malthi continued to make garlands. Every once in while I looked into the living room to see what kind of progress Dhiren and Naveen were making with the altar. When the tea was ready they sat in some chairs near the kitchen.

"How much sugar do you want, Malthi?"

"One teaspoon," she replied.

"You Dhiren?" I asked.

He put up two fingers. "Two."

"How much sugar do you want in your tea, Naveen?"

"Three teaspoons," Naveen replied.

"Bhiaya wants his tea as sweet as sugar candy," Malthi teased.

I laughed because I knew my husband loved his tea, very sweet.

The tea break was short and Malthi's teasing was forgotten as the preparations continued.

"Come with me upstairs," Naveen said to me, "Let's select the pictures we should bring down for the puja."

"All right," I replied.

Naveen and I talked as we mounted the stairs and entered the prayer room. Our thoughts and conversation was focused on selecting the right Sathya Sai Baba photographs for the celebration. Then I saw it.

"Naveen look! There is misri on Shirdi Baba's statue!"

There were more than one hundred pieces of small, rectangular sugar candies, approximately 1/2 inch by a 1/4 inch, on and spilt around the statue Ashu had given us the year before.

"We were just talking about sugar candy downstairs and here Baba gives us sugar candy for the tea." Naveen declared.

*~ "I always think of him, who remembers Me. I require
no conveyance, carriage, tonga, train, or areoplane. I
manifest Myself to him, who lovingly call Me."*
Shri Sai Satcharita pg. 212

Moments later Malthi and Dhiren came upstairs and witnessed this sweet event. I never knew when and how Baba would make his presence known. He consistently surprised me with His omnipresence.

The following day an enthusiastic crowd of one hundred and fifty people attended the celebration. Bhajans were sung, and what had come to be his scheduled time, 30 minutes after bhajans began, Baba graced us with His presence. Lockets, necklaces, and bracelets, among other things, including sugar candies, vibhuti and kumkum, dropped from the carnations Baba rapidly rubbed between his fingers and lovingly gave to everyone.

After the entire crowd was blessed, it was time to cut the birthday cake. One candle was set in the middle of a white cake with orange writing that said, 'Happy 79th Birthday Sathya Sai Baba'. Without saying a word, before he cut the cake, Baba took his index finger and changed the 9 on his cake to 8 to make it 78th Birthday. In India, the tradition is to write on the cake the age the person is going to be in the coming year. In the western culture, we use the age the person has completed. Baba showed He follows the tradition of where He is, therefore in South San Francisco He was 78 years old. Sai Baba stresses He does not want us to change our religion, culture, or traditions. Whatever you sincerely practice or believe He wants you to continue. That's all. God is in everything and every place.

At this point in my journey with Sai Baba I had come to accept so many things I never thought would be a part of my life. I had come to accept that Shiva, Sathya Sai Baba, and Shirdi Sai Baba are the same. I had come to accept that anything was possible, that the miracles that were occurring in our house and Malthi's house and in the mandir were real, including Baba coming into Malthi turning Malthi into Baba. So when Rao came to me after he had a vision in December, 2004 saying that I should write a book about Baba manifesting through Malthi, you would think I could have accepted that task easily...I could not.

One day after bhajans Malthi made an announcement, "Everyone, keep good notes of what you are experiencing with Baba in this mandir. You can give your notes to Anita for a book."

Malthi announced to the devotees that I would be writing a book! When I heard her it was almost like a joke to me. I laughed at the very thought of taking on the task of writing a book...a book with such a complex subject!

A couple of weeks later during bhajans I took the issue of my writing a book to Baba. I turned to Dhiren, who assisted Baba whenever He came. It was within this time frame that Baba actually began to speak.

"Dhiren, can you please ask Baba if He could give me the strength and knowledge of how to write the book on Baba?"

I asked Dhiren to ask because I simply couldn't ask the question.

Dhiren did as I requested.

Baba laughed. "You are asking Baba to write about Baba?"

I didn't know how to respond. I simply looked at him.

"Ye-es," Baba continued, "it will happen."

I believed I would write a book about Baba because He confirmed that I would, but I had no idea how.

Manifested misri after Naveen
requested sugary tea

CHAPTER EIGHTEEN

Some of the things that I experienced through Baba are stuck in my mind as if it happened yesterday.

On January 20, 2005, bhajans were being held downstairs. It was a temporary location because the mandir was being remodeled upstairs. I walked in that evening and saw Malthi and Geeti sitting on the sofa.

"Sai Ram," I said, and took a seat close to Malthi.

A few minutes later Malthi put her head down as if she were sad or sick.

"Are you okay?" I inquired.

Malthi responded by making the okay symbol with her hand, but less than five minutes later she got up and went upstairs.

"Should I follow her?" I asked Geeti softly because bhajans were in full swing.

Geeti motioned that I should, and I realized as I left the room Geeti was close behind me. We climbed the stairs. When we reached the top we saw Malthi sitting in the dark on a sofa that was near the mandir door.

"Open the puja room?" she ordered.

I went over to the door but it was locked. Dhiren kept

the door locked because he was remodeling the mandir. "It's locked," I informed her.

Malthi got up and forcibly wriggled the knob. "Why is the door not open?" she screamed. "Go get Dhiren. Tell him to come and open the door."

I wasted no time getting down those stairs and returning with Dhiren. Immediately he unlocked the door but he did not go in. Instead he remained beside Malthi. What I should say is he remained beside Baba, because by then we all knew Baba had come.

I felt somewhat frantic considering how Baba had come, and how He demanded that I open the locked puja door. So I wanted to appease Him and I ran downstairs again.

"Ashu, hand me Baba's white cloth and scarf," I said hurriedly.

Ashu asked no questions. He quickly gave me Baba's clothing.

With Baba's white cloth and scarf held tightly in my hand I rushed up the stairs again. I was about to put them on Baba but He was staring off into the distance in such a way that I didn't want to distract Him. By then Parvati Auntie had joined us.

Suddenly Baba shouted, "Leave! Go downstairs!" His voice was full of rage.

That was all I needed to hear. It was the same for Geeti and Parvati Auntie. We started back down the stairs.

"Anita. Geeti. Stay here," Baba ordered.

I stopped in my tracks. I could tell Baba was very upset. More angry than I had ever seen him in the five years that I had been coming for bhajans.

"I am going to le-eave this house," He shouted. "I have no respect here. Everyone is testing me!" He began to pull out His hair. I mean pull it out! A plug of hair was dashed to the floor.

Next, Baba broke the gold necklace that hung around His neck and threw it down. I didn't know what to do. I stood there helplessly as Baba tore at his cloths until they were ripped apart.

The fear that ran through me at that moment…I can not put into words.

"What do you want to see?" he continued to demand. "I'm not attached to anything. What form do you want to see? You all keep making mistakes. All of you."

Geeti and I were terribly frightened at Baba's display of temper.

"Forgive us, Baba," I pleaded.

"Yes, please, Baba. Forgive us. We do make mistakes," Geeti made her apology, our words did not quell Baba's anger. He continued to rip at his clothes. There seem to be nothing we could do to appease Him.

Then Dhiren spoke for the first time. "I made mistakes, Baba. Please forgive me."

Baba's gaze bore into him. "How many times will you continue to make the same mistakes? You keep making mistakes and asking for forgiveness." The air vibrated with His voice. Suddenly Baba pointed at the mandir, "Are you going to make this mandir?"

"Yes, Baba. I am," Dhiren replied.

Baba looked at him with steely eyes. "I am giving you a final chance to change."

"Please Baba," Geeti continued to plead, "forgive him and all of us. We all make mistakes unintentionally. We are your children," she beseeched Him.

Thirty minutes must have passed before Baba totally calmed down. He pointed toward the unfinished puja room, indicating that we should go inside. Of course we did.

"Open the curtain," Baba said.

Before we sat down we opened the curtain that sectioned off the original mandir. It teemed with a plethora of Gods and Goddesses.

Baba took a seat. He pointed at Mata's picture. I looked at the picture of Durga Mata and then I looked back at Baba. When I looked at Baba this time His tongue was extended. It was at least five inches long! I was astounded because I felt as if I was looking at Kali Mata! Who else could it have been but Kali Mata with a tongue elongated in such a way? This is an image I will never forget. Never.

Baba left Malthi's body and we were all left in shock, including Malthi.

"What happened?" Malthi said when she saw her torn clothes and her necklace on the floor.

We attempted to explain to her what had taken place, but remember all this time there were devotees downstairs waiting to do puja. So what did Malthi do? As her life has demanded since Baba started coming, Malthi quickly adjusted. She rushed into her bedroom, changed her clothes and put on a white bandana. The next thing I knew she had re-joined the bhajans.

Malthi's voice that night was something to hear. When Malthi sang she sang with such sincerity and power, and when the flower she held in her hand filled with vibhuti she shared it with everyone.

Now when I look back at this event I can't help but think about how Shirdi Sai Baba was also known for his bouts of anger. I guess I was blessed to experience this as well.

Mata in Shree's Mandir

CHAPTER NINETEEN

Through the years the fact that Baba gave darshan in South San Francisco spread inside the USA and to various places around the world. It became difficult to accommodate the crowds, especially during popular celebrations such as Shivaratri, Easwaramma Day, Guru Purnima, Shirdi Sai Baba's and Sathya Sai Baba's birthdays. At times the attendance reached as high as 500 and more. Devotees stood and sang bhajans throughout the house as they waited for Baba's darshan. It was the only way the mandir could accommodate such crowds. Once they were graced with a one-on-one darshan of Baba… meaning a devotee could come up and ask questions if they chose to, or if not they would simply kneel before Baba and receive whatever He chose to give them. After that the devotee would rotate out of the main mandir to allow devotees who had not had darshan the opportunity. It was because of the large numbers that created a spatial challenge that the Lal family decided to expand the mandir and the seating area.

The expansion plans included three life size marble statues of Durga Mata, Shirdi Sai Baba, and Shiva; the result of the generosity of many of the Sai devotees. Dhiren constructed a marble altar base for the murtis. Because of their weight and size they were brought into the mandir through an adjacent window and put on top of the marble base. Once the murtis were in place he built the altar around them and framed the entire platform with an intricate, customized woodwork. When the renovations were complete the new seating area could easily accommodate one hundred fifty people.

While the mandir was being remodeled the veil of mourning for Ram Lal Uncle lifted in January 2005. Celebrations that had not been held in the mandir for a year resumed.

To mark the installation of the statues a Murti Sthapana Ceremony, The Placing of the Sacred Image Ceremony, was held on March 4, 2005. Several priests conducted the vedic rituals. This was a very important event. Through powerful ritual the Gods and Goddess were welcomed to reside inside the statues. Although we know God is omnipresent, this Murti Sthapana Ceremony was an agreement between the Deities and us, the devotees, that Durga Mata, Shiva and Sai Baba would come into the mandir, come into the murtis, and in exchange we would care for them and do service for others, *seva*.

The resultant awakening, the moment when the Deity descended and could see through the eyes of the sacred image, was catalyzed by the use of a gold instrument smaller than a toothpick. That golden tool was rubbed across the lower eyelids of Durga Mata, Shiva and Shirdi Sai Baba's eyes to open them...it brought them to life.

On and off throughout the powerful, twenty-four hour ritual Baba graced us with His presence. That day, sometimes Baba would mix and smoosh food with His hand and pass it out to the devotees. He spent time talking with us; joking with us. It was a day of high celebration.

Through the years Rao like several others became very active in the mandir. They helped prepare and maintain the space for pujas and bhajans. One day he shared an event that totally astonished him.

"Anita, something very fascinating happened the other day when I was changing the clothes of the murtis."

"What happened?" I asked, magnetized by a different kind of timbre in his voice.

"I was putting the finishing touches on Baba, and I came to His bandana. I tied the bandana on very tight and I used a safety pin so it would not come off. The next thing I knew Malthi came running from downstairs holding her head. She was breathing very hard; inhaling and exhaling like she was in pain. 'Take off the bandana. Take it off!' She ordered me to take it off. So I took it off immediately," Rao was emphatic. "As soon as I removed the pin and released the bandana Malthi was relieved. Then Dhiren was there and he gave me a hair clip to secure Baba's bandana. He also asked me not to use the safety pin. And do you know later that day Malthi had vibhuti sprouting from her head! Lots of it. They collected it in a big container. There was also vibhuti coming from her feet. Both of them."

I was also amazed by this. "It's all Baba," was all I could say.

"Yes it is," Rao agreed. "Then when Baba came He told me it was kind of me to decorate Him but to do it very gently." Rao paused. "I think it was the safety pin that was causing Him pain."

Activities continued at the mandir. The number of devotees continued to increase and so did Rao's experiences.

"Anita, my sister, this is something you are going to find very difficult to believe.

Now I had known Malthi for four years by then, and there was very little, if anything that I would find difficult to believe, but from the expression on Rao's face he had experienced something he believed would challenge me.

"I was in the mandir cleaning up for the Hanuman puja. Malthi was in the mandir with me. Suddenly she asked me to bring her the dry coconut that had been offered to Baba. It was half a coconut. So I gave it to her, and she sat there and ate it. But I noticed she was eating it rather strangely. Malthi was eating like a monkey."

With that statement Rao definitely got my attention. "Do you mean...?"

"No wait." He put up his hand and motioned for me to listen. "Then Malthi asked me for a banana. By then I was thinking what is going on! But of course I gave her a banana." He shook his head. "And Anita, she peeled that banana and ate it like a monkey would eat it. Right before my eyes a transformation was taking place. It may have taken all of fifteen minutes, but I saw it. As a microbiologist I know a person cannot will their body to change. For my body to change it can not be brought on by my just wanting it, but I tell you Malthi's body changed. Her lips became dark red and turned downward like a monkey. And her lower face around her mouth began to protrude like a monkey's face sticks out."

I tried to picture what Rao was describing but I must say it was very difficult.

"Malthi pointed toward her mouth and asked me to touch it. I was stunned by what I was seeing, but as a scientist I was also extremely curious. So I touched her lips. When I touched Malthi's mouth it was not soft. It was nearly as hard as a statue, but it was also rather tough. Later I realized that Malthi's face had turned to the face of Hanuman ji."

Rao had been right; accepting Malthi's transformation into Hanuman ji was difficult to believe.

Later that year Sarita was one of the fortunate devotees who Baba told who she was while He was alive in Shirdi, India.

"When I approached Baba tonight," she said, "He asked me 'Do you want to know who you were in a past life?' I was surprised by His question but of course I answered, "Yes'. 'You were Laxmibai,' Baba told me."

After that an ongoing drama unfolded between Baba and Sarita. For three weeks in a row Baba asked her, "Do you have my nine silver coins?" Sarita had no idea what He was referring to and she began to ask other devotees if they understood Baba's question. Eventually Sarita was told before Baba took Maha Samadhi He gave Laxmibai, a deeply sincere devotee, nine silver coins as a symbol that she had steadfastly adhered to the nine fold path of **bhakti** and seva. Once Sarita understood she had nine small, silver coins fashioned by a silversmith. When the coins were ready she gave them to Baba.

"I gave Baba the coins," Sarita explained, "and He put them in a piece of cloth and tied it with a knot. I know Baba was satisfied that I gave Him the coins because He never asked for them again."

Sarita's return of the nine coins initiated an annual ritual around the same time each year during which Baba took out the coins and washed them with yogurt, honey and such.

~ *Nine Forms or Types of Bhakti:* Shri Sai Satcharita pg. 112

1) *Shravan (hearing)*
2) *Kirtan (praying)*
3) *Smaran (remembering)*
4) *Padasevan (resorting to the feet)*
5) *Archan (worship)*
6) *Namaskar (bowing)*
7) *Dasya (service)*
8) *Sakhyam (friendship)*
9) *Atmanivedan (surrender of the self)*~

Shirdi Sai Baba: Malthi reacted when Rao
used a pin to tighten His bandana

CHAPTER TWENTY

For at least three years Geeti and Kumar Jayasurya had been coming to Malthi's house. Geeti was one of the kindest, most compassionate women I had ever met. I knew she and Kumar had a deep desire to become parents, but that was something that had evaded them. One day Baba said to Geeti, "You will become the world's greatest mother." At the time we did not know Baba was telling us that Geeti and Kumar would soon adopt a daughter from India. There was loads of joy when Saisha joined the Sai family, and for a year their daughter brought Geeti and Kumar much happiness.

Because we were a close group I heard that Geeti was scheduled to have minor surgery in September 2005. I was not alarmed by this because from what I had been told Geeti's procedure would be a simple one. I did not enquire any further about it to respect her privacy.

A few weeks before the surgery something strange occurred during bhajans. Normally Baba remained seated in His special chair in front of the crowd. We would approach Baba during darshan. Through the years Baba's seat had evolved from Baba sitting on the floor, to a banquet-like chair with metal arms, to a decorative upholstered chair with wooden sides, to His present chair, a beautiful stationary seat; a gift from Malthi's Canadian relatives who brought it down in a van and assembled it piece by piece.

This particular day Baba rose from His seat and dashed to the back of the room where Geeti sat on a chair. He spoke directly to her then returned to His seat. We did not know what was said. Baba's words were for Geeti and Geeti alone.

As usual we celebrated Shirdi Sai Baba's birthday with a grand puja, at the time Geeti was recuperating from her surgery. When I saw Kumar after the celebration I asked about her.

"How is Geeti, Kumar?"

"She is ok," he replied, "but she has slight fever."

I thought nothing more about it. I mean…I was satisfied with what Kumar told me because I believed fever was a normal part of her recovery process.

The next morning I received a phone call from Malthi.

"Anita…Geeti is not doing well," she informed me.

I thought of how I felt my conversation with Kumar had established Geeti was on the mend. "She's not?"

"No," Malthi replied. "They transferred her to ER. We are going to Peninsula Hospital. Do you want to come with us?"

"I want to come," I replied, "but I'm going to have to join you later as soon as I am done with my errands."

We hung up, and about an hour later I hurried to the hospital. When I arrived I joined Kumar, Malthi, Ashu, and Parvati Auntie in the emergency room. Their expressions were not encouraging.

Frightened, I asked, "What is wrong with Geeti?"

"She is in a coma," Malthi replied.

Mathi's response was totally unexpected. A coma! *But it was a minor procedure,* I thought.

Moments later a doctor came out to update us on Geeti's condition. His words hit me like a ton of bricks. "We are trying our best to revive her," is all I can remember him saying.

Suddenly Code Blue blasted over the intercom and the doctor who was talking to us rushed back to ER. Everything was happening so quickly. The next thing I knew the hospital staff was gathering us together in a private room. I knew what was about to happen but I could not believe it was happening. In my desperation I turned to Malthi.

"You are my Baba," I said to her. "Please save Geeti." I shouted and began to cry. "If you are our Baba you can save her!"

Malthi acknowledged me with a compassionate look but she focused her attention on Kumar.

"Kumar, look...would you like to see Geeti in a wheel chair for the rest of her life? Would you like to see her living like vegetable?" she asked him, ignoring my cries.

But I would not let her ignore me. "Why aren't you doing something?" I challenged.

That's when Malthi turned and looked at me. "Anita. Please do not worry. Baba will do what is best for Geeti."

It wasn't what I wanted to hear...what I needed to hear. "She just got Saisha! Saisha needs her mother more than anything," I pleaded.

Malthi could not take anymore. She just couldn't. She rushed out of the room, walked down the hall and exited the building. I followed her. I watched Malthi as she got in her car and sat inside. I knew she was praying for Geeti.

I didn't know what to do so I stood and waited at that door. Finally, in what may have been five minutes, Malthi joined me. Together we returned to the room.

One of the doctors was not far behind us. In a very

professional manner I watched him walk over to Kumar. Gently, the doctor touched his shoulder. "Geeti has passed away," he said softly.

With those words the doctor confirmed our greatest fear. We were already crying; when we heard his announcement our emotional dams broke. Within twenty-four hours burial arrangements were made to have Geeti put to rest according to her family's Buddhist beliefs.

Geeti made her transition on Saturday. By the time Baba gave darshan the following Thursday, in light of His presence in our lives, I was having a very difficult time accepting her death. And Baba knew it.

After Baba came and situated Himself in His chair He motioned for Kumar and me to come forward. I felt rather nervous as I rose from the floor, but I also wanted an answer to the question that plagued me…Why did Geeti have to die?

Baba went straight to the point. "Why are you crying?" He asked after Kumar, Saisha and I had kneeled before him.

I didn't say anything. Nor did Kumar.

"Do you know she was suffering for eight years?" Baba's piercing question stunned me. "Do you know she had cancer? Do you know what cancer is?" His relentless enquiry vibrated the air. "Do you know what radiation is?" His gaze penetrated our very being. "I could have brought her back but she would have been in pain and brainless."

Baba paused. His eyes continued to penetrate us. "I had a conversation with Geeti three weeks ago. She wanted to be a mother. I fulfilled her wish. She was the world's greatest mother." He paused again. "She wanted to have a child to leave behind for Kumar. Saisha is Durga. She is my child." Baba focused on Kumar. "If you want Geeti I have to take Saisha back." This was the truth Baba spoke. "Kumar, you have to be strong for Saisha otherwise I will take her. I know you have lost everything but I will be with you." Then Baba spoke to Saisha in a Sri Lankan language before he addressed her father again.

"Kumar, Saisha will take care of you. Geeti is in heaven and you all," Baba pointed at the entire crowd, "are living in hell. She is in peace with me; there is no pain and no suffering for her. When I spoke to her three weeks ago Geeti did not want to live in pain any longer. She made the appropriate arrangements before she went for the surgery."

It was a life-jarring exchange with Baba. As I retuned to my seat the realization of the things I did not know was uppermost in my mind. I did not know Geeti had cancer. I did not know she had been suffering for so long. I did not know the things Baba spoke of. I was a mass of emotions and one of them was guilt. I wished I had visited Geeti in the hospital when she first had her surgery; but there is nothing you can do with that kind of regret. From it all I surrendered to one thing. Baba knew what was best for all of us. He knew our past, our present and our future. Because of the love I knew Baba possessed for us I accepted the way Geeti made her transition, and I accepted the timing of her transition was the best it could be. The ways of Divinity are unfathomable. The more I experienced the more deeply I understood.

Current Mandir

GAIN AND LOSS, BIRTH AND DEATH,
ARE IN THE HANDS OF GOD.

Shirdi Sai Baba

CHAPTER TWENTY-ONE

My father, Mohinder Pal Bawa, had a stroke in April 2006. It was his very first major illness. All of his life he had been a very healthy person, so this was a major shock for the entire family. For two weeks after the stroke he was involved in rehabilitation, and it appeared he was making a slow but steady recovery. I tried to be at my father's side as much I could during his difficult time, and I must confess the feeling of having Baba so near was pure nectar. I consulted Malthi many times concerning my dad's health.

~I am ever living to help and guide all who come to me, who surrender to me and who seek refuge in me.~
Gyarah Vachan

On May 6th I attended a twelve hour bhajan session celebrating the life of Sathya Sai Baba's mother, Easwaramma. During the Easwaramma Day celebration Baba came and went. At times it would be Baba and at other times it would be Malthi attending the festivities. I arrived around noon, but my father who had been placed in a rehabilitation center was foremost in my mind. No sooner I had arrived when Baba called me forward. He gave me a white carnation and some kaphour, a small, square piece of camphor. Then Baba pointed eastward. "Go. Light this and circle with it seven times." I knew He was telling me to go to my father.

When I arrived at my father's care facility there was pure chaos in his room. Lots of my family members stood by helplessly as my dad appeared to be hallucinating. He talked about things we didn't understand and his movements were jerky and chaotic. It was clear something was terribly wrong.

I looked around the room and said, "Please everyone leave the room."

Perhaps because they didn't know what else to do, no one objected to my request.

When my father and I were alone I lit the camphor Baba gave me. With the lit kaphour I walked around my father's bed seven times. Instantly the room was inundated with the powerful smell of camphor. After I carried out Baba's instructions I realized I still held the white carnation He gave me in my hand, so I placed it under my father's pillow. Within moments, my father calmed down.

As I watched my father come back to himself, I could not help but think how Shirdi Sai Baba was in South San Francisco, but He knew my father was having another stroke in Creekside Nursing Home in San Pablo, nearly thirty miles away.

Baba continued to ask about my dad's health and He ensured me that my father would be okay. One thing I must say is, over the years I witnessed how Baba was very open and honest no matter the depth of the situation. Although Baba told me my father would live, He also said my dad would be disabled for the rest of his life. I accepted that, and Baba's words have proven to be true.

"It is all Baba's lila," is a phrase that is very often associated with Sai Baba. In June 2006, one of the greatest lilas that I have witnessed began to unfold in South San Francisco. I was among a small group of close Sai devotees with whom Malthi shared a request; a request that was made by Baba. Baba wanted Malthi to have another child. I had no idea why Baba would make such a request, but He expressed His desire although He knew physically, Malthi would have a very difficult time conceiving. Any doctor with access to her medical history would say it was impossible.

After Baba's request bhajans became the time when Ashu and Dhiren would ask Baba, "How can we make this happen? Who will carry the child?" They were the voice of our collective concern because we had no idea how this physical impossibility would become reality.

One day someone asked, "Baba, why don't you create a baby?"

Without hesitation Baba replied, "Yes I can, but I don't want to break the law of nature. This baby is important for the sake of appeasing nature, so that mankind will continue to enjoy a sense of wellbeing and prosperity. This area will be badly affected by disasters if this baby does not come."

For me it meant Baba was warning the Bay Area, which everyone knows is a prime earthquake zone, that we would experience the forecasted disasters if the baby He named Shivam did not come.

Over the next few months many volunteers offered to be surrogate mothers, but eventually it always fell apart.

By now there were hundreds of devotees that frequented the mandir, and because of the renovations that were completed the previous year, there was plenty of room to accommodate the crowds. The number of manifestations also increased, and the types of objects that appeared and how they appeared increased in variety. Many Sathya Sai Baba devotees are aware that in Prashanti Nilayam for many years He produced a Shivalingam from His mouth every Shivaratri. One evening during bhajans I experienced Shirdi Sai Baba producing a Shivalingam from His mouth in South San Francisco.

I watched from the back of the puja room. It was obvious that Baba was about to produce something from His body. To our amazement what appeared was a Shivalingam! It was approximately two inches tall and an inch and a half in diameter. That was the first of several Shiva lingams that Baba produced orally within a relatively short period of time. I can't help but believe there was an energetic connection to the baby, Shivam, Baba had asked for.

Actually, Shivam was the most profound thing Baba requested, but He also asked for something else during that period. Bakul was involved in the mini-drama.

"Baba asked for His chillum," Bakul said as he looked at Malthi, confused. "What is a chillum?"

I had no idea what a chillum was, so I simply stood there.

"It's an old style smoking pipe." Malthi made a disgusted expression. "I don't want to smoke that. Don't get it."

That was the first time Baba asked for his chillum. When bhajan time arrived the next Thursday, Baba came.

"Did you get my chillum?" He asked Bakul.

"No, Baba," Bakul replied. "Your daughter told me not to get it. She doesn't want to smoke it."

"You get me my chillum," Baba repeated to Bakul.

Bakul found himself in a fix after bhajans. "Again Baba told me to get His chillum."

"Well, you can get the chillum," Malthi acquiesced slightly, "but don't put any tobacco in it."

The following bhajan Bakul brought a hookah for Baba.

"Did you bring my chillum?" Baba asked.

"Yes, Baba," Bakul replied enthusiastically.

"Did you bring tobacco?"

Bakul's spirits sank. "No, Baba. Your daughter said not to."

"You bring me tobacco," Baba admonished him.

Four weeks from Baba's initial request for his chillum, Bakul fulfilled his entire request. The very first time when Baba smoked the hookah I could tell He was content.

"From this day on," Baba said to Bakul, "you must prepare my hookah every Thursday. It is your job."

Shirdi Sai Baba's chair when He "comes". His "chillum" is on the left near the base.

CHAPTER TWENTY-TWO

Through the years I heard various names of Malthi's extended family members. Some still lived in Fiji, others in Canada and in California cities not far from South San Francisco. Some relatives knew that Malthi literally became Baba while others knew there was a connection between the two. Some believed...some did not.

In September, 2006 Malthi's immediate family made a trip to Calgary to attend a wedding. Not long after they returned to California I met Uday Narayan, a cousin of Malthi's. I found out Malthi and Uday grew up together in Fiji and were very close as children, and those feelings remained although Uday lived in Canada.

When I met Uday at Malthi's home, the day before Shirdi Sai Baba's 168th birthday celebration, he was extremely ill. You could look at him and see that. With tears Uday shared his story.

"When Malthi came to Calgary for the wedding she saw me and asked, 'What happened to you?' I told her I didn't know. I told her I have blood coming from my mouth and nose and from other openings in my body. And when I look at something that is very near it looks like it is very far away; almost as if it is fading away." Uday paused. "I also told Malthi I went to Royal Columbian Hospital to get some help. They ended up giving me some pills to take. One pill twice a day; a total of 3,060 milligrams of medication," his sincere gaze attempted to focus on my face, "but they didn't tell me what was wrong.

"The next day after the wedding my father held a puja for Mata. While I was there, Parvati Auntie told me that I needed to come to another relative's home. That I would be able to talk to Baba there. Now I had no idea to what extent Baba was present with Malthi. I knew there was something. What?" He shrugged slightly. "I really didn't know. But I went to the house with some other family members, and I was very surprised to see that Baba had come into my cousin." Uday teared up. "Baba was very straight with me. He said, 'I am not going to twist this around. I will get straight to the point. You've got Stage 3 pancreatic cancer and you have three months to come to Shirdi in South San Francisco. After that, do not bother to come.' We were all crying by then. And so," Uday swiped at his tears, "I went back and talked with my brothers and sisters, cousins, friends…and everybody pulled together to give my wife, Ajeshni, and me fares to come here." Tears continued to accumulate in Uday's eyes. "I don't know what is going to happen to me."

Later that day, downstairs at Malthi's house Uday tried to relax. He felt very weak because he had bled for seven hours. Yet he still tried to socialize with the family. While Uday drank a beer and talked to Malthi, Baba came.

"Do you know any bhajans?" Baba asked.

Uday began to cry and tried to sing a bhajan but it was difficult to sing in such an emotional state.

"Don't worry," Baba comforted him, "Drink your beer.

What would happen if you were getting healed right now?" Baba enquired.

Uday heard what Baba said but he didn't understand.

"Will I be healed, Baba?" Uday asked.

"Don't ask those questions now, Shirdi Sai Baba replied. "Wait until tomorrow night."

The next night I saw Uday go up to Baba after Baba came during the birthday puja. Uday cried as Baba sat in front of him intensely smoking the hookah. After Baba turned the pipe over to Bakul He manifested a rudraksha bead from a carnation and gave it to Uday. "I am giving you a new life."

Uday returned to his seat on the floor not far away from where Justin played a double-headed barrel drum. All the while Baba continued to look at him with a concentrated gaze.

Later Uday said, "As I sat there the room was getting very smoked up from Baba smoking the hookah again. He was taking my pain away when He was smoking the pipe. Then I began to feel like someone was blowing furnace heat on me. It was hot! So hot I turned around to look for a vent or something because I was trying to see where the heat was coming from. But I didn't see anything." He took a deep breath. "Then I began to feel the heat inside my body. It came in through the top of my head and went inside my stomach. I was very aware of it." Uday touched his abdomen. "After the heat entered my stomach it went into my left leg first, and then into my right leg and out my toes. It was a very powerful feeling. I knew when it left my body. This heat, whatever it was, left my body out of my toes and after it left my body it left the room. I am certain of that," his tone was emphatic. "I could feel it. And by the time the puja was over I felt like a new man. I felt ten years younger and stronger. The next morning I put on some shorts and went outside because all my symptoms were gone. I had no more bleeding! None. I cried while I stood there because I knew I was healed.

~If you cast your burden on me, I shall surely bear it.~
Gyarah Vachan

But an interesting thing happened the next day. I was about to eat and I had some food in my hand. At that moment Malthi, who had taken a shower, came down the stairs. She could barely walk straight. My cousin looked like she was in a lot of pain." Uday swallowed. "Then all of a sudden Baba came. He began to speak in Tamil." He threw up both his palms. "I don't understand Tamil. Baba took a roti from my plate and he began to eat it.

Parvati Auntie was there and she said, 'Baba, tell me why my daughter is in so much pain?'

Baba answered her in Hindi, 'Do you want to know whose pain she took? My daughter took his pain.'

Mathi took my pain," Uday said. "I was no longer in pain but she was. I have been free of pain and bleeding ever since the puja."

I AM IN EVERYTHING AND BEYOND.
I FILL ALL SPACE.

Shirdi Sai Baba

CHAPTER TWENTY-THREE

Some may think with all the amazing spiritual phenomena that blanketed the Lal family's life, they wouldn't have everyday concerns such as creating an income to support themselves. They would be wrong. As a result, the family opened an Indian grocery store in the Fremont area in 2007. It was definitely a family affair. The entire family worked hard to establish the business.

When summer dawned they prepared for the grand opening. Flyers were distributed and the day arrived with many Sai family members attending the grand occasion. I had to work that day but Ashu told me what happened.

"An elderly man was the first customer to enter the store. He bought incense and that seemed to break the ice," Ashu said, "because after his purchase more customers arrived. Baba had promised that He would be the first customer," Ashu's eyes gleamed. "So actually Baba made an appearance twice that day. It wasn't long before Baba came through my sister."

"Baba came to the Grand Opening." For me, it was a novel thought.

"He did," Ashu said. "When He came we prepared a special

place for Him to sit and we gathered around Him. While He was there Baba produced a Laxmi murti."

"From a carnation?" I asked.

"No," Ashu replied. "From His mouth."

I thought of the physical discomfort Malthi sometimes experienced after Baba produced objects from His mouth. Sometimes her throat was sore for two days or more. "How big was it?"

"About two or three inches tall."

"That's big." My hand automatically touched my throat. "That was a nice grand opening gift for store," I said

Ashu shook his head. "No-o. Actually it was for one of the Sai devotees who lives in the Freemont area."

"Amazing." I was a little surprised by that. "Only Baba knows His lilas."

From my perspective, if I have not stated a greater truth in this book, that is the truth. Only Baba knows His lilas.

A year passed. Baba produced a total of ten Shivalingams during that time, but Shivam, the baby, had not been born and that did not sit well with Baba.

"I want Shivam," He said. "Why can't you bring me, Shivam?" Sometimes He appeared to be quite angry because we could not produce the one thing He really requested. Baba had given us this task and He wanted us to accomplish it. It was obvious Baba didn't want to do it. It was for us to do. Why? Perhaps there was some kind of karmic benefit in it? I do not know.

From the time I came to know Baba to the year 2007, there were substantial changes in the dynamics of the Lal family household. Many long time devotees had come and gone for various reasons. The breath and depth of some of these occurrences rippled throughout the Sai family for good and for bad, but through it all Baba continued to come. He never withdrew His presence. The truth is we were all being challenged on many levels, and I recall Baba saying this about the advent of Shivam.

"Man makes all these social rules and there is a place for them. But when it comes to this, when it comes to Shivam being born and the purpose for his birth, I don't care about man's rules. You...man says this is wrong and this is right. I don't. I don't differentiate between right and wrong. I treat everyone the same. Rich or poor. Murderer or hero."

I've thought about Shivam and Baba's insistence that this baby must be born and how He did not care about social rules. Baba's utmost concern was for the welfare of mankind as a whole. The context of an event makes all the difference. A man kills another man on the streets of South San Francisco and it is called murder. A soldier kills another soldier in a war and he is considered a hero. A life has been taken in both scenarios. Context and perspective are key.

God knows past, present and future. When and if He judges, He knows the Big Picture; when we judge we judge from a mere sliver of what is the truth.

Shivaligams from Shree Sai Baba of
South San Francisco's mouth

I AM THE SLAVE OF MY DEVOTEE.

Shirdi Sai Baba

CHAPTER TWENTY-FOUR

Two thousand and eight arrived along with Baba producing another Shivalingam from Malthi's body, and an endless flow of devotees and their problems were laid at Baba's feet. Through His will they were solved.

Sarda, Rao's wife, experienced Baba's omnipotence in 2008 during a very troubling time for their family.

"We had an issue with immigration," she said one evening, "so Rao decided that I should go back to India with our daughters and he would stay in the States. This is not what we wanted but we didn't see any other choice." Sarda paused. "Of course after Rao's decision I was very concerned and I decided to ask Baba about it. So when Baba came two weeks ago I asked Baba, 'Am I going back to India?' He said, 'No, your green card will come within fifteen days.' And Anita," her eyes brightened with joy and amazement, "we received the green card today in what looked like junk mail! Today is exactly fourteen days later! We are so thankful to Baba for keeping our family together. But I must admit I am surprised that Baba knew that we would get our green cards within fifteen days."

Parvati Auntie had seen and experienced countless miracles

through the years, but when her daughter began the tell-tale motions of something being manifested through her mouth in mid-2008; Parvati did not know what to expect.

"I could tell something was about to come," she said. "Then Malthi opened her mouth and I could see it emerging, but the moment I saw it I got the fright of my life! It looked like a serpent! But when the lingam was out I saw third eye markings on the stone. That's what confused me. Coming out of her mouth the colors of the third eye markings looked like a serpent's eye," Parvati Auntie explained. "This is the eleventh Shivalingam. Baba said Shivam will come next."

An energetic connection between the Shivalingams and Shivam was confirmed by Baba.

Finally, Baba told Parvati Auntie the baby would be born from Malthi. We knew that would be a major medical miracle, and all we could do was wait to see what would happen next. The Sai family had tried every way we knew to bring Shivam, and by this time we were exhausted in every possible way.

I was scheduled for a business trip to Chicago in October, 2008. I decided to visit the Shirdi Temple while I was there, but before I left I wanted to ask Baba about it. I asked Him the Thursday before I was scheduled to leave for Illinois. As usual after I approached Baba I touched His feet.

"I'm going to visit the Shirdi Temple," I informed Him.

"Are you going to Shirdi?" Baba asked, innocently.

"No, I'm going to Chicago, Illinois."

"Yes, you will see me there," He replied. Then Baba blessed me by giving me a carnation.

I went back to my seat as Baba called Naveen forward. Later Naveen was adamant about the things Baba said to him.

"Baba does not want you to travel for one year after this trip."

I laughed. "Why-y?"

Naveen didn't laugh. "He said it is not good for your health. Baba basically said your life could be in danger if you travel alone after this trip. And after hearing what Baba has said I really don't want you to go to Chicago at all."

"But Baba said this trip was okay." I replied, and a couple of days later I travelled to Illinois for business. While I was there I visited the Hampshire Shirdi Sai Temple. When I returned to South San Francisco on several occasions I asked Baba when I could travel again. Baba eventually put an end to my questions.

"I will tell you when the time comes." He pointed his index finger at me after I made another inquiry. "Do not ask me again."

It was difficult not to travel because I truly enjoyed it at that point in my life, but I didn't ask Baba again.

Diwali, the Festival of Lights, arrived, and it was celebrated in a big way at Malthi's house. Eighteen Sai Families attended the festivity which began with approximately thirty minutes of prayer in the mandir. Once the puja was over food and beverages were served downstairs. As always the party was lively and everyone was having lots of fun. Before they knew it Baba came! Soon after His arrival He asked Rao to dance for the crowd, and he did; accompanied by enthusiastic claps from the crowd.

Once Rao's dance was over Baba quietly said to Rao, "Go upstairs."

Once again Rao did as he was told. When Rao entered the mandir he could not believe his eyes. Excited, he rushed back down the stairs as Baba made this announcement.

"We will celebrate Diwali as we did in Shirdi."

"Yes!" Rao said, eagerly. "Come upstairs and see what Baba has done."

Everyone climbed the stairs. To their surprise the mandir was decorated with many lit *diyas*. These were not the decorative tiny clay pots that you find in the stores today, but the diyas that were used when Shirdi Sai Baba was present in Shirdi. Baba had created the entire Shirdi style celebration; historic diyas and all. Two vertical rows of diyas were lined up in front of Ganesh who was seated on the floor. After the amazing event everyone descended the stairs, and Malthi, who had returned said, "There were eighteen families here tonight, and Baba created eighteen diyas; one for each family."

These are the kinds of special gifts we received from Baba.

MY EYE IS EVER ON THOSE
WHO LOVE ME.

Shirdi Sai Baba

CHAPTER TWENTY-FIVE

"You do Mata's Puja," Baba instructed me one day in December, 2008. And so...we did. Naveen and I launched 2009 by preparing for Mata Chowki at our home. It was to be held on January 2nd. Our biological family members and members of our Sai family were invited. Red was the theme for the puja, and a variety of red saris and *churanis*, a kind of decorative wedding cloth, were used to decorate the altar. When the preparations were complete Durga Mata sat in the center of the three tiered altar. Below her Shirdi Sai Baba presided, followed by a luxurious Laxmi and Ganesh, along with another image of Durga. The bottom level of the altar showcased the *jhoti*, a light surrounded by fruit, flowers, sweets and money.

As a part of the offerings to Mata, Naveen and I offered a red sari, as ***Mata Shingar***, and something else I was rather uncertain about, an artificial jewelry set which included a necklace, earrings and a tika. Deep inside I felt giving Mata artificial jewelry wasn't right, and I pledged after that puja I would never give her artificial jewelry again.

That afternoon, five performers arrived and set up their

musical instruments and acoustic equipment. About an hour later approximately one hundred attendees trickled in, and dinner was served before the puja. It wasn't long before bhajans were enthusiastically initiated by two designated performers: one male and one female. After they launched the singing with their beautiful voices all of us actively participated.

At some point during the session I noticed Shruti was crying. I took her upstairs so she could play with the other children. Although she is known to be an aspect of Vaishnavi; she is still a child. When I returned to bhajans Shruti returned with me. I could feel the energy in the room was very powerful; undoubtedly increased by our songs to Mata; songs that we sung from our hearts.

"Jai Mata-ki!" resounded throughout the crowd. "Jai Mata-ki!" "Victory to the Goddess," we shouted.

It was wonderful to be a part of such a moment, and I was grateful to Baba for allowing us to play a key role in bringing it about.

With such a mindset I turned to Malthi, who sat beside me, and said, "I would like to see Mata today." I have never said that kind of thing befor,e and I have no idea why I said it... perhaps it was an extension of my gratitude.

Malthi smiled and continued singing. A few minutes later she replied, "You are Mata."

I smiled at Malthi before I looked at Durga Ma's picture which was the focal point of our altar. What I saw there should have taken me by surprise. There were nine Mata's surrounding the main figure. Those nine Durgas were not on the physical picture, but I saw them nevertheless. After that I must confess I don't recall what happened. Later I was told by those in attendance that I glowed... and smiled... and said, "Mata is here." If what they tell me is true, as Malthi said, the energy of Mata was present in me; something to this day that I have not wrapped my arms around. I was also informed that Mata's energy left me and entered Shruti momentarily before She left the room and went up the stairs.

We sang bhajans that night until midnight. When bhajans were over some attendees left while others remained behind. Pockets of conversation took place throughout the house and tea and snacks were available for all who wanted them.

Everyone had enjoyed the Mata Chowki, and Naveen and I were pleased that we could provide a space for such a special occasion. In the midst of the lingering crowd Malthi approached me.

"Your house is blessed with Mata's grace," she said. "Go upstairs to your prayer room and see."

Of course I was the first to climb the stairs to see how Mata had graced us, but I was not prepared for what I saw. On Durga Mata's brass statue which is approximately seven inches tall and six inches wide was a large amount of kumkum and...almost an exact duplicate of the jewelry set Naveen and I offered to Mata at the beginning of the puja! I am saying that necklace and earring set materialized on Durga Mata. In that materialization was a specific message for me, because the moment I saw the jewelry I understood that Mata had accepted our "artificial" necklace and earrings. God only cares about the sincerity of your heart; not what the offering is made of.

About a foot away from Durga Mata kumkum had also materialized at Ganesh's feet. By the time I saw Mata's blessings most of the attendees had left. So it was only close friends and family members who shared that special moment with me.

The bounty of Mata's blessings spilled over into the following day when I returned to Baba's room to light a candle. For some reason I felt there was something in the pile of kumkum at Ganesh's feet. Call it a curious nature, but I took my index finger and gently dug into the red powder. There was something there! A one and a quarter inch high Ganesh with sixteen arms! Veera Ganapati had also materialized, and he too was made of brass. To live a life so close to Baba means to constantly see the impossible made manifest.

Shruti when Mata came to Anita's Mata Chowki

Materialized necklace and kumkum on
Mata murti at Anita's Mata Chowki

CHAPTER TWENTY-SIX

When Baba sanctioned it, from time to time Malthi visited the homes of selected Sai family members. In the early years the process was not stringent, but as time progressed and the number of devotees increased Baba became more selective. The truth is wherever Malthi goes Baba is present; if He decides to show himself more fully or not is up to Baba. But basically this means when Malthi enters the home of a devotee Baba will most likely come; along with manifestions of vibhuti, kumkum, murtis and **chandoor**. Those who are present and fortunate enough to experience this receive special teachings and personal information from Baba. This information may range from talks about spiritual discipline to who the devotee was when Baba was alive in Shirdi.

On March 3, 2009 Rao attended a Sai bhajan at a house warming of a devotee in Freemont, California. Malthi also attended.

"I didn't see you at the house warming, Anita. It was Tuesday before last," Rao said.

"I know," I replied. I could tell Rao was excited. "But we couldn't come. We had family obligations."

"Oh." His eyes sparked as he nodded with understanding. "Well, Baba came. And when He was comfortable in front of us He pointed to me to come forward. I was kneeling before Baba and He had this very kind expression on His face. And then He gave me a loving slap on my cheek and said, 'I will give you better than this house.' And this was a nice house, Anita," Rao injected. "Do you know three days later, last Friday, I received the house lottery as a first time buyer! We got to pick a house! We chose a four bedroom three bath house!"

"When did you enter the lottery," I asked, amazed at his good fortune.

"Five years ago we placed our name in the lottery system, and in just three days Baba drew our number! His words are extremely powerful, Anita. We are so thrilled with joy that Baba has given us this house."

~ There shall be no want in the house of my devotees. ~
Gyarah Vachan

Three weeks later the Sai family celebrated Malthi's 40th birthday with a grand party. It was Baba's idea. Actually we were uncertain about holding the party that had been planned for many months because there was so much going on…so many challenges, but Baba insisted.

"The party should be held for my daughter."

That is what Baba called Malthi, "his daughter". I had come to learn Baba's words were set in stone, and as he foretold six months earlier about four hundred guests attended the magnificent affair. At the celebration Ashu read a beautiful poem that he wrote for Malthi that summed up how many of us felt.

Our Sister

God gave a gift to the world,
The day she was born.
A person who loves and cares so much,
Without a single thorn.
She always sees a person's needs,
And fills it as best she can.
Who encourages and lifts people up,
With her soft, gentle hand.
She touches each life she enters,
Like a breath of fresh air.
The look of her beautiful smile,
Is enough to show how much she cares.
She is worth more than any jewel,
A heart of pure gold.
Seated in our hearts,
A place she will always hold.
She is a special treasure,
For all that she has done.
May the love she has shown others,
Return multiplied in sums.
Tonight is your chance,
To shower her with that love.
As we ask you to join us in celebrating,
Her birthday has come.
We ask you to come forward today,
As we celebrate her birth.
May it be a night to remember,
Forever on this earth.

But even in the midst of parties and celebrations Baba continued to ask for Shivam.

As the quandary over how Shivam would be brought into this world continued to hound some of us, in February of 2009 I found myself in a Kaiser emergency room. They diagnosed me with vertigo, and the physician recommended that I not fly until my condition improved. Why? Frequent flights exacerbate vertigo and could cause flare ups. I was shocked to hear the doctor basically advise what Baba had told me four months earlier.

Needless to say I did not travel for any reason for one year. That year was full of challenges for so many of us, but Baba continued to come and devotees continued to come to the mandir.

FULFILL ANY PROMISES
YOU HAVE MADE.

Shirdi Sai Baba

CHAPTER TWENTY-SEVEN

In April 2009, Rao became very solemn during and after bhajans and I found out he was deeply concerned about the son of a friend.

"What is his name, Rao?" I asked.

"Har Kamal. He was in a terrible motorcycle accident," he replied with deep distress. "Har is a young sikh man barely twenty years old; just one year older than my daughter. They grew up together. His condition is very, very bad. I spoke to the doctors. They say he has no chance of surviving. He has severe head injuries, a broken arm, ribs and now he is in a comma." Rao looked down before he continued. "Sarda and I rushed to the hospital to see him when we heard he had gone into the comma, and I asked his father if we could place Baba's vibhuti on him. He gave us permission to do that, and we put vibhuti all over his body. I want to help them so badly." He shook his head. "We have visited him everyday since then and we have placed two pictures; Baba's picture and Dwarkami's photo in the ICU room where he is. We are all praying day and night for Har's recovery but there is no sign of life. And Anita, for the last three weeks during all of this I have come to bhajans and Baba will not look at me or talk to me. I even placed Har's picture on Baba's lap…on the murti. I am very depressed watching this young man lie there with no life." Rao inhaled. "His parents are praying day and night to Guru Nanak ji. Har is the only son they have.

"I am sorry to here this, Rao," I said most sincerely. "But of course Baba knows."

"Yes," Rao nodded. "I know."

During those weeks when Baba came He washed His face with milk and **Haldi**; one of the methods he used to heal someone, but those actions were just another aspect of so many things Baba did.

The following Thursday, Baba called Rao forward and asked, "Do you have faith in me?"

"Yes, Baba," Rao replied without hesitation.

"Do not go home," Baba said. "Go to the hospital."

He handed Rao a red flower that I eventually found out was for Har.

Rao told me, "The next day around 4 p.m. I got a phone call from Har's father, who was at the hospital. He was extremely excited. He told me both of the pictures that were hanging on the wall fell on Har Kamal's head and there was this bright light around him. After that happened Har moved his fingers and opened his eyes! Overjoyed I rushed to the hospital. When I arrived there the doctors and nurses were waiting for me. I wanted to tell me about a miracle that had happened! Har had moved his fingers and opened his eyes!"

Har Kamal's brush with death was another medical miracle I was privy to which involved Shirdi Sai Baba. As time passed Rao said Har made a total recovery.

One Thursday, during the summer, I prepared a list of questions to ask Baba about Shivam. As soon as Baba came to give darshan I was the first to go forward. I held the list as I touched his feet, leaned in and started to speak, but before I could Baba said, "I know you have a lot of questions but I am not going to answer them."

But because Shivam was such an issue I wasn't deterred. "Baba," I began, "I know you want Shivam to come, but we need your help. How can we bring the Shivam? Can we just adopt a child and bring it to you to get your blessing?"

I could tell from the expression on Baba's face that he wasn't happy with me or the situation.

"I thought you were smarter than that," He said. "Why do I have to give you all the details? I thought you could figure it out yourself."

I just stared at Baba. I didn't know what to say to that. Baba had been asking for the Shivam to come for years and his frustration over our inability to bring the Shivam was very apparent.

"Now I need to do something and I don't care about your cultural traditions." His face set like stone. "What you consider to be wrong or right; I don't care about that. I will take care of this. Shivam needs to come… and he will come."

Very quickly I returned to my seat in the back of the mandir. I had no idea what Baba would eventually do, but I knew Shivam would come. I had absolutely no doubt in Baba's ability to create a miracle to bring him, if that is what Baba chose to do. From countless experiences I had come to accept this world as Baba's lila.

At the end of bhajans some close Sai family members approached me to find out how Baba responded to my list of questions.

"Baba knew I had made a list of questions," I told them, "but he didn't want me to ask anything. I managed to ask a couple of things that came to my mind," I tried to explain, "but now Baba says he is taking charge of bringing the Shivam. So I know it will happen now," I said with confidence. But for me many questions remained because the dilemma of Shivam's advent had been going on for three years. But now, I knew Shivam would be born…somehow.

That September was a month of beginnings. Out of the blue Baba selected Naveen to be a Gurmukhi, which means to be his disciple. I had always considered Gurmukhi a part of the Sikh tradition, and I felt Naveen was selected for the position and not me because Naveen always saw Shirdi Sai Baba as his guru. It was the first time Baba had selected a Gurmukhi and Naveen felt honored. I was sincerely happy for him.

September will forever stand out for me because it was also the month when I, along with a few others, was told the good news that Shivam was on his way. I discovered Malthi would be the divine mother. Finally, Baba's request was going to be fulfilled. I can't tell you how happy we were, and now when I look back rather naive in a way. I say that because I now know in order to bring a divine being into the physical world, into this world of Maya…illusion, an amazing energetic store house must be present within the mother. Over the months I witnessed how that extraordinary presence manifested in Malthi. Did I understand everything I experienced? No. Did I have questions? Absolutely. But the bottom line was Shivam was on his way.

I LOVE DEVOTION.

Shirdi Sai Baba

CHAPTER TWENTY-EIGHT

We celebrated Shirdi Sai Baba's 171st birthday on Saturday, October 3rd, and as I witnessed through the years this birthday celebration also brought abundant material manifestations, and a crowd of at least four hundred who were blessed with Baba's darshan. During this birthday celebration I received a special gift.

When I knelt before Baba He said, "I know you have been waiting for my response a long time. Yes…you can travel now," words that were nectar to my ears. It had been a year since Baba, and later my physician, advised me not to fly and I adhered to the advice. But as soon as I returned home that night I booked a flight to attend a conference in Bethesda, Maryland.

The following days overflowed with work and I continued to attend the weekly bhajans. Now, with the increase in the number of regular attendees, there were many people that I did not know. The mandir and devotees had changed through the years. It was almost as if there was a finite amount of time that devotees were allowed such close proximity to Baba. I say that because I saw so many come and go. Many that I thought would never leave; and the question loomed in the back of my mind, *When will our time come to an end?*

Months passed as we waited for the birth of Shivam. During the celebration of Sathya Sai Baba's birthday which was held on Saturday, November 28th, Naveen received Gurmukhi along with five other members of the Sai family. The celebration of divine births continued when Baba decided a baby shower for Shivam would be held at our home on December 19th. As always Naveen and I felt it was a great honor to hold these events, and we combined the shower with our annual Christmas party. Nearly two hundred people graced our home that day and at the end of the party, when the majority of the crowd had left, Baba came. We gathered around Him in the living room, and to my surprise Baba made an interesting request.

"Anita, bring me some tandoori chicken."

"Baba, would you like that with rice, dal and chipati?" I asked.

"Whatever you want to add," He replied.

So, I brought Baba a meal with tandoori chicken. He accepted it and said to me, "Have some chicken."

"No, thank you, Baba," I said.

"I know you don't eat meat, but it's okay."

I still declined, and Baba invited everyone to partake.

Suddenly, Baba spoke a series of numbers but no one knew why. Then he began to talk to us on a variety of subjects from spiritual lessons to personal topics. When He was done Baba announced, "I gave you the lottery numbers."

A gasp reverberated through the group, followed by exasperated statements like, "What were the numbers?" "Do you remember the numbers?" To our dismay no one remembered all of the numbers and no matter what we said or did Baba did not repeat them.

Before he left that night Baba blessed all of us. But He did something very intriguing as He stood at the main entrance of our home. First He stretched His arms out to His sides; then Baba raised them until His hands touched the top of our door. I watched as Baba traced the outer edges of our door, from the top down with his hands, and when He reached the bottom He balled His hands into fists. "I am taking all the problems from your home with me and leaving only happiness."

Baba appeared to be very happy that Shivam's event had turned out so well. That was the last day in 2009 that we saw Baba.

CHAPTER TWENTY-NINE

Shivaratri arrived February 13th, 2010. Several priests from all over the world officiated the ceremony at Malthi's house. The mandir upstairs and a large open space downstairs were filled to capacity with devotees.

After the ceremony I met a woman named, Gwyn McGee. I was excited to meet her because I had just finished reading her book, *Bharosha Ma: 22 Weeks With Divinity*, and I wanted Gwyn to autograph it. It amazed me that she was attending the Shivaratri celebration in South San Francisco. According to the information in her book she lived in Atlanta, but here she was in California. To me the timing of meeting her was a little uncanny.

Because the things I read in her book struck me in such a special way I invited Gwyn to my home. I wanted to talk to her. I wanted to talk to her because I was intrigued by her book and her writing. Without hesitation Gwyn accepted my offer, and we shared a leisurely chat in the pleasant night air as we walked. Within minutes after leaving the mandir Gwyn was seated in my dining room enjoying a cup of tea. We discussed her book which focused on Bharosha Adhikari, a Nepalese woman, who died and recalled how Sathya Sai Baba came to the other side and brought her back. Gwyn wrote about the time she spent with Bharosha Ma, and Bharosha Ma's new life that is filled with miracles because of her special connection to Sathya Sai Baba.

Soon our discussion turned to the subject of writing, and the conversation was extremely invigorating. I felt very comfortable with Gwyn, and before long I shared something with her.

"Years ago Baba gave me permission to write a book about Him."

"Really?" she replied.

"Yes." I smiled. "Maybe that is why Baba sent you here… to help me with it."

"Maybe." Gwyn smiled and shrugged simultaneously. "I've experienced enough with Baba to know anything is possible. And it is mighty strange that I've been in San Francisco for only two weeks and I right away I'm directed to this mandir, and now I'm meeting you."

"So how long will you be here?" I asked.

"One year," she replied. "Out of the blue my husband received a one year assignment in San Francisco. We were very surprised."

~Sai Baba often said that- let His man (Devotee)
be at any distance, a thousands kos aways from Him,
he will be drawn to Shirdi like a sparrow, with
a thread tied to its feet.~
Shri Sai Satcharita pg. 146

Now I was truly surprised. "Maybe Baba has brought us together. Maybe **you** will write a book."

She shook her head. "Noooo. Maybe we will write one together."

We laughed.

Then Gwyn continued. "We will have to wait and see what Baba has in store."

CHAPTER THIRTY

From that night forward, every Thursday after bhajans Gwyn came to our home. Naveen and I shared our Baba experiences and she shared her experiences with us. Over time it came to feel as if we had known each other a very long time, and we looked forward to our Thursday visits.

One Thursday, March 11th, 2010 after bhajans, Gwyn and I along with a small group gathered in the mandir around Malthi. She sat in a chair in the center of the room.

"Baba said he will give darshan in five weeks," Malthi announced.

"In five weeks?" Someone questioned. "What date is that?"

A quick calculation was done.

"April 15th," Malthi said. "Tax day."

We all laughed. We didn't know what it meant. Baba had promised He would not give darshan until after Shivam was born, and Shivam was not due until some time in the beginning of May. I thought it could possibly mean that either Baba would give darshan for the first time in months, or Shivam would be born, but I didn't tell anyone. Well…at 2:25 p.m. on April 15th, tax day, Shivam arrived.

~See, to keep My words, I would sacrifice my life, I would never be untrue to My words.~ Shri Sai Satcharita pg. 213

A couple of interesting events happened that day according to news sources on the internet. A massive fireball, in other words, a meteorite was seen streaking across the mid western sky; states where the phenomenon was reported included Iowa and Wisconsin. Second, in Wellington, New Zealand a two foot statue of Shirdi Sai Baba was found six to seven feet underground when a developer was digging for construction purposes. Water sprung up from the spot where the statue was buried, and that water slowly developed into a small pond. Now that Shirdi Sai Baba statue is floating safely on a small pallet, and the developer decided to develop elsewhere.

There are no coincidences when it comes to the Divine. Baba said he would give darshan on April 15th, and he gave it through the birth of Shivam. The birth was announced in the heavens in the form of a meteorite and in the earth when Shirdi Sai Baba's statue was unearthed.

Shree and Shivam

CHAPTER THIRTY-ONE

For four months, while we waited for the birth of Shivam Baba did not give darshan in South San Francisco. On April 23rd Baba decided to come again. I was not there but during our regular after bhajans visit I experienced it through Gwyn, who excitedly shared her very first darshan of Shirdi Sai Baba.

"Baba came tonight," she said before I could welcome her and close the front door.

"He did?" I replied.

"Ye-es! A few years ago during an interview in Puttaparthi Sathya Sai Baba was questioned by one of his American devotees about not coming to the United States, although it had been rumored many times that Baba was coming. The devotee asked Baba when would He truly come. Baba's response, "I come to America all the time. I come to South San Francisco.""

"See, Baba has confirmed what is going on here," I replied pleased to hear this confirmation from India. "How was your experience tonight?" I asked.

"It was something else," she said looking into thin air. "I was sitting four feet away from Baba's chair in the front of the mandir, but before he came I was also sitting behind Shree at an angle, and I could see her face vey well."

Gwyn called Malthi Shree. The majority of the people who come to these Sai bhajans call Malthi Shree, which is her real name. Family and some who are close to her refer to Shree as Malthi.

"I noticed Shree was staring off into space," Gwyn continued. "Then her face began to change. I could see the corner of her mouth descend downward."

"It doesn't look like Malthi because it is more of Baba's face," I said.

"It didn't look like her," she replied. "And what is the young man's name who appears to be taking care of things? He arranges the flowers and accepts the garlands, and even places the prasad on the altar."

"Ashu," I replied. "His name is Ashu."

"Yes. Him. He came over to Shree and began to remove her lipstick with this cloth."

"Yes. Baba requested that things like make-up, earrings or clips in her hair be removed. Even her bindi. Baba doesn't like those things but Malthi loves them."

"How interesting," Gwyn replied. "Shree's mother went up to help Ashu and there was another guy."

"Bakul."

"Bakul." Gwyn nodded her head with acknowledgment. "He started to light this hookah."

"Baba asked for that too," I told her.

"Wow. Well, I guess when the hookah was ready Bakul went over and joined Ashu and Shree's mom as Ashu began to put this white garment on Shree."

"On Baba."

She nodded in agreement again. "Yes. When that was done,

Ashu placed a white bandana on Baba's head and Bakul placed his finger in the back of Baba's head so that Ashu could tie it, and tighten it."

She was so excited by what she had seen, and was determined to recount every detail.

"Garlands were placed on Baba's wrists and a large garland was placed around his neck. I was fascinated to see Baba lift one of the garlands on his wrist to his nose and smell it. Then he took those flowers and made a motion like he was cleaning the tip of the pipe before he inhaled it."

"Baba always does that," I said.

"Do you know why he smokes the hookah?"

"To cleanse the environment. Baba uses a flavored tobacco in the hookah."

"Many indigenous cultures use a spiritual tobacco to cleanse themselves and the environment during spiritual ceremonies," Gwyn noted the similarity. "But Baba must be heavy because they seemed to have a difficult time getting him up off of the floor."

"Ye-es. It's a big task. Baba is very heavy."

"Hmmm. I wonder why?" Gwyn asked but she did not wait for an answer. "They gave Baba this walking stick and struggled to get him over to His chair. That was really something to see. He walked like an old man, kind of stiff like and," she paused, "he does not look like Shree."

I shook my head. "It is not."

"You're right." She looked deep into my eyes. "Because I watched Baba and He seemed to settle His body, or should I say settle into His body until He found a comfortable position. Actually during that process. Baba placed his right leg over his left leg. Just like you see Shirdi Sai Baba sitting on the stone."

"That's Baba favorite position," I told her.

"Interesting. I've seen Him sit like that many times in photographs and paintings," she replied. "And after He was sitting like that Baba looked as if He was adjusting His vision through Shree's eyes. Then the next thing I knew He looked directly at me, and for a split second He blessed me with his right hand...the Abhaya mudra that Sathya Sai Baba is known for, before He turned it over with His palm up, and then curled His fingers and motioned me to come."

I was very impressed with how Gwyn remembered all the details. I guess being a news reporter for several years and a writer for nearly twenty has a lot to do with her attention to detail.

"When I was up there, Anita, I don't remember if I said anything. But I know Ashu handed Baba a white carnation as Bakul gave me this quarter sheet of typing paper. So I held the paper below the flower as Baba began to rub the carnation rapidly between His fingers. Vibhuti started coming out. There was a lot of it. And me being the cry baby that I am I started to cry. Oh my God, tears were falling on the paper wetting the vibhuti.

I laughed at her. "Must have been joyful tears for seeing Baba for the very first time."

"Definitely," she replied. "I just couldn't believe I was having such an experience. I have never seen Baba come in this way before. I have seen a lot of His miracles because of Bharosha Ma, but I have never seen Him come through a human being like this," Gwyn explained. "After that I went back to my seat and 'lo and behold' maybe fifteen minutes later Baba leaned forward toward me with His thumb pressed against His index finger. I knew He wanted me to place my open palm beneath them. So I did. And guess what? These little squares of sugar candy dropped into my palm." Her eyes widened. "I felt so special, and I felt they were so special, and I thought I'm just going to hold on to these. So I continued to sing bhajans with the candy in my palm but it began to melt. I mean turn into pure clear syrup!"

I giggled at her story.

"I guess it was melting because it was freshly made by Baba and the heat from my hand was melting it! I never would have thought of that. So I panicked and I quickly placed the remaining pieces in the paper with the vibhuti that Baba had manifested for me."

That night was a special night for both of us.

As the months passed Gwyn shared many first experiences with me, including how Baba threw a carnation to her during the Easwaramma Day celebration. When it gently fell into Gwyn's lap a large two sided Shirdi Sai Baba pendant rolled out. It is a beautiful ornament. One side has rhinestones surrounding the image of Shirdi Sai Baba in an orange robe juxtaposed against a stunning green background. Ashu told Gwyn, through the years he noticed Baba manifested jewelry that matched the colors the recipient was wearing that day. Gwyn was wearing the exact green and orange when she received the pendant. There are no stones on the opposite side of the ornament which features a more traditional rendition of Baba wearing dark orange with a black backdrop. Slightly, Gwyn's pendant reminded me of the pendant that simply materialized in our prayer room one day. When? Naveen nor I truly know.

The subject of writing a book seriously cropped up in a conversation Gwyn and I had as my sabbatical approached.

"I've decided I'm going to write the book about Baba during the two months that I'm off work," I said. "And when I decide to do something, I do it," I proclaimed to help convince myself I could do it. "Do you want to help me?"

Gwyn wasn't convinced that Baba wanted her to be a part of the project.

"Unless Baba gives me direct instruction to do this I don't believe it's for me to do. You're the one with the notes, and He told you directly. Baba has made it clear to me before when I am to do something." She shook her head. "Sooo, I just don't want to get involved unless He wants me to."

Well…in short order, perhaps two weeks later, Gwyn had a dream. In the dream Gwyn was told by a disembodied male voice that she would help me write. The voice said, "You will help Anita write. You will help her explain the past."

Next, a woman named Jan Fredrick who received a spiritual communication forecasting Gwyn's writing of *Bharosha Ma: 22 Weeks With Divinity*, resurfaced in Gwyn's life after several years. Jan told Gwyn she would write another Baba book. At that point I said, "We will ask Baba on His birthday."

Now we have come full circle. As you read in the beginning of this book, I arrived late for Baba's birthday celebration. And as I had intently prayed for as I rushed from Santa Cruz to South San Francisco I found Baba was waiting for me. The hundreds of devotees had received darshan and I was practically the last one. When I knelt before Baba I asked, "Baba, do Gwyn and I have permission to write the book?"

"Yes," He smiled before He pointed toward Gwyn in the crowd. "I already advised her. I will guide you in writing the book." With those words Baba gave His permission.

After I touched Baba's feet I sat beside Gwyn as the celebration continued. He launched our journey that night with carnations blessed with orange sindoor and misri, and the writing of *Shree Shirdi Sai Baba Of South San Francisco* began.

Pendant manifested for Gwyn
from this carnation

AFTERWORD

by

Anita Bawa

It is hard to believe that I was able to put my notes into this book. It was a wonderful experience working on this book and of course, realizing it was guided by Shirdi Baba.

I look back ten years; I am a different person from the person who always wanted to achieve in the academic and business world. I never thought that one day I would talk about God's miracles. I grew up in a Hindu family where we prayed to Lord Shiva and were taught that we must have good conduct and values, and we were taught to be good human beings. I learned at a young age: non-violence, be truthful, be honest, be patient, be of firm character, be compassionate, have moderation in eating, and be pure internally and externally. In our home we were always reminded to help the needy, feed the hungry, and to give back to our community. We were told that is your sadhana or puja.

On my spiritual path I learned to watch my thoughts because they become words and words become actions, those actions become your destiny. I also learned that happiness is within us and good and bad situations are created by our thoughts. If we are feeling sorry for ourselves during the bad times, take the opportunity and learn from the situation. I believe each hardship is a teaching which makes us stronger and we appreciate it when we look back. There are always positive and negative situations and we will not be able to differentiate between them if we remain in one condition. For example, we need sun and rain, day and night.

Recently, I was reminded by one of my friends that 90% of the things are in our control based on our reaction to the situation. I am a firm believer that a person with a positive attitude is always a winner, because he or she will manage any situation or calamity.

During this spiritual journey I learned more about other religions and that they all lead to the same road. They all teach to be kind to all beings because God resides in all of us. It is important that we must have unconditional love and compassion for all of humanity.

While I was writing this book I discovered there is no time and space for God's miracles. I learned about dream symbols; that things happen for a reason and we may not know the reason at that time. Although the situation may look bad or sad, after time passes and you look back; you realize there was a good reason why it happened.

In September 2010, my husband and I went to Mount Shasta, which is located in California. Prior to our trip we did not know that Mt. Shasta was a spiritual place. We just wanted to go for hiking and to see nature's beauty. We learned that no one goes to Mt. Shasta unless the mountain calls you. It is considered as sacred a mountain as Kailash Mountain in India. We had a wonderful spiritual retreat, and there was so much love and energy in the air. It appears this trip was made for us by Baba to experience His presence. We met four ladies who had been coming to Mt Shasta for years. They had knowledge about many different beliefs, and they were highly educated in the medical field. They shared their experiences of God's miracles with us.

One of them had a near death experience where she was returned to earth to practice Buddhism and to teach others. Another was a prestigious university professor who could talk to dead people. From the Mt. Shasta trip I learned that this kind of phenomena could happen anywhere in the world.

After reading the book, The Fourth Dimension by J. Jagadeesan, it is confirmed that spirit...trance mediums do exist, and they are special beings. These God forms that come are responsible for various aspects of activities: wealth, education, health, etc.

I would like to conclude that ten years ago all of this was foreign to me, and I did not have a clue that this kind of phenomenon actually existed. After watching with my own eyes where there is no greed or benefits, I realized it must be God's grace on those special beings who can trance into another dimension to heal people, provide guidance with their personal lives, and guide their spiritual path.

I am thankful to God for giving me the opportunity to share my experiences.

AFTERWORD

by

Gwyn McGee

To think human beings are capable of knowing the entire range of scenarios created by the Divine to reach humanity at this crucial time in our spiritual evolution is a mistake. Summing up the Divine in His/Her many forms and modalities is beyond our mental, physical and spiritual ability. I believe what we are experiencing in this Kali Yuga is more holographic than anything we can conceive of; that the Avatar makes His presence felt in innumerable ways that can, and do have powerful impacts on vast numbers of lives. Because a belief or occurrence does not fit into our personal paradigm of possibilities has nothing to do with what the Avatar is capable of, and what He is willing to do to obtain His objectives for our spiritual growth and well being.

On September 28th, 1990, the birthday of Shirdi Sai Baba, Sathya Sai Baba spoke about His previous incarnation.

"All that Baba said or did was for the good of the devotees alone. Towards the end, Abdul Baba came to Baba. Baba told him, "I shall appear again and give darshan.""

"When will that be?" asked Abdul.

Baba told him, "It will be after eight years."

The first advent of Sai was in Maharashtra. The second advent will be in Madras," Baba said. "It should be noted that when this form (Sathya Sai) made Its advent, Andra Pradesh was part of Madras Presidency. When He was asked in what form the next advent would take place, Shirdi Baba told Abdul Baba alone: "I will give darshan in the name of Sathya for upholding Truth." That is the present advent.

The two bodies are different, but the Divinity is one. The first advent was for revealing Divinity. The second advent is to awaken the Divinity (in human beings). The next advent is for propagating Divinity. The three Sais are Shirdi Sai, Sathya Sai and Prema Sai.

Bodies are transient. These vestures are assumed only for the sake of devotees. Unless the Divine comes with a form no one can develop faith in the Formless. The Divine in human form is the preparation for comprehending the Formless Absolute."

That day in the Prashanti Mandir, Sathya Sai Baba was quoted as saying, "It is not easy, therefore, for anyone to understand the ways of the Lord. When one cannot understand the ways of the Divine it is best to keep silent and at least refrain from indulging in grievous misinterpretation. Seek, therefore, to understand the ways of God and through devotion and worship strive to experience the Divine."

In South San Francisco we are being allowed to experience the Divine through Shree "Malthi" Lal in a way that is unique and precious. Can I logically explain my own experiences or the experiences Anita and others shared with me? No. But logic is not powerful enough, not expansive enough to explain the Divine. Did the events and conversations described on these pages take place? Outside of a few liberties taken with when and how the conversations occurred because this is a collaborative work between Anita and myself…absolutely.

Yet, with all the Divine unfoldings it does not mean everything that occurs in Shree's life and in the lives of those who are close to her, or who come to the mandir are perfect. Karma still exists. Baba can and does bestow His grace at His discretion, but the Wheel of Karma continues to turn creating events in our lives as we have karmically earned.

Maya is alive and well in South San Francisco. We have encountered her in many ways; as a beautiful, energetic Being and as the abettor in the illusion of the perpetual human dramas that flow through our lives. Because Shirdi Sai Baba comes to northern California Maya's illusion is that much more powerful. She is a part of Baba, and as a result Maya amuses us; discourages us; shocks, inspires, loves and disappoint us; and she also brings us joy. I believe the karmic duty of anyone who is fortunate enough to come close to the physical aspect of this Divine play, be it in South San Francisco or Puttaparthi, is to strive to remain centered in the midst of it all. We should strive to play our roles as best we can, and to be the ultimate observers of our own lives, so we may grow spiritually while we participate in this earthly school. Focusing on a physical form of the Avatar, Sai Baba, or being physically close to it may be one of the greatest Divine lessons of how not to be attached to the form.

At the time this book was published Uday Narayan does not take or need medication, and Shivam's life bears proof of his connection to Shiva as Baba foretold. Shruti can manifest vibhuti in the carnations she is given after bhajans, and devotees like Ashu's spiritual vibration has been increased where he too experiences Baba's divinity in unique ways. Parvati Auntie's prayers are so powerful she can persuade a reluctant Apsara to continue to grace us with her presence on earth, and Anita's spiritual dharma continues to be made clearer day by day. What I have seen in South San Francisco is this: Baba's devotees are the actors in His divine play, and our spiritual lessons and karma determine His script.

As an author of two books that give tiny glimpses of the beauty, the majesty and the mystery that is the Avatar, Sai Baba, my desire is to remain worthy of the unusual dramas I have been privy to witness. I do not understand all that I have encountered; I no longer try. But this is how I feel. Through the use of the fathomless instrument of my heart, my experiences with Sai Baba are pure experiences with a boundless Love…a love that motivates the Infinite to place Itself in a finite form to benefit human-kind. By all I have experienced I continue to be amazed, and I am…and will be forever grateful.

Jai Sai Ram, Prabhu! Jai Sai Ram! Victory, My Lord! Victory!

Anita Bawa has 20 years of experience in the biotechnical field and is currently a Senior Manager at a leading biotechnology company. She received her Bachelor of Marketing and Management degree from Saint Mary College and a Master in Business Administration from the University of San Francisco.

Gwyn F. McGee is the author of 13 novels under the pseudonym, Eboni Snoe, and the non-fiction, *Bharosha Ma: 22 Weeks With Divinity*, employing her real name. She is a former journalist occupying positions from radio street reporter to News Director, and TV anchor. Gwyn is a speaker and spiritual seeker. www.gwynmcgee.com

GLOSSARY

Aarthi - a Hindu ritual in which light from wicks soaked in ghee (purified butter) camphor or another suitable oil, is offered to one or more deities

Amrit - a substance with a consistency similar to thin honey and a flowery, sweet taste

Bhaini - Sister

Bhajan - devotional singing

Bhakti - loving devotion

Darshan - viewing of a deity

Dhuni - Hindu practice of creating a sacred site or focal point for a particular spiritual purpose

Ghee - clarified butter that remains when butter is melted, boiled, and strained

Lilas - the plays that God as an Avatar creates on earth

Loka - a specific plane, sphere, domain or dimension of awareness that is at the same time a living dimension of divinity

Maha Samadhi - the conscious abandoning of the physical body of a great being

Mandir - a place of worship associated with Hinduism

Misri - sugar candy; rectangular shaped sugar crystals

Mudra - an arm or hand position that expresses an attitude or action

Murti - sacred image

Paduka - silver sandal

Prasad - Anything, usually edible, that is first offered to a deity, saint, perfect Master or the Avatar, and then distributed in His/Her name

Puja - prayer; prayer ceremony

Satsang - a gathering during which spiritual matters are discussed; a gathering that involves the singing of Indian devotional songs

Seva - service for others

Shivalingam - an egg shaped stone that holds ... represents all of creation; the cosmic egg

Shri Sai Satcharita - an important source about Shirdi Sai Baba; written in Marathi in 1916 by Govindrao Raghunath

Sindoor - a powdered substance ranging from pink to orange; a red or orange powder used to dot the forehead of Hindu women, also applied during wedding ceremonies to the center part of the bride's hair

Vibhuti - a grayish ash manifested by Sai Baba as a form of a blessing; a sacred ash used in Hindu ceremonies

Made in the USA
Lexington, KY
07 December 2011